KT-195-405

WITHDRAWN

Marketing your Complementary Therapy Practice

LRC Stoke Park
GUILDFORD COLLEGE

Visit our How To website at **www.howto.co.uk**

At **www.howto.co.uk** you can engage in conversation with our authors – all of whom have 'been there and done that' in their specialist fields. You can get access to special offers and additional content but most importantly you will be able to engage with, and become a part of, a wide and growing community of people just like yourself.

At **www.howto.co.uk** you'll be able to talk and share tips with people who have similar interests and are facing similar challenges in their lives. People who, just like you, have the desire to change their lives for the better – be it through moving to a new country, starting a new business, growing their own vegetables, or writing a novel.

At **www.howto.co.uk** you'll find the support and encouragement you need to help make your aspirations a reality.

How To Books strives to present authentic, inspiring, practical information in their books. Now, when you buy a title from **How To Books**, you get even more than just words on a page.

STEVEN A. HAROLD

101 TRIED

AND TESTED

WAYS TO

ATTRACT

AND RETAIN

CLIENTS

4TH EDITION

Marketing your Complementary Therapy Practice

howtobooks

615.50688 HAR

184811

Published by How To Books Ltd,
Spring Hill House, Spring Hill Road, Begbroke,
Oxford OX5 1RX, United Kingdom.
Tel: (01865) 375794. Fax: (01865) 379162
info@howtobooks.co.uk
www.howtobooks.co.uk

How To Books greatly reduce the carbon footprint of their books by
sourcing their typesetting and printing in the UK.

All rights reserved. No part of this work may be reproduced or stored in an
information retrieval system (other than for purposes of review) without the
express permission of the publisher in writing.

The right of Steven A. Harold to be identified as author of this work has
been asserted by him in accordance with the Copyright, Designs and
Patents Act 1988.

© 2011 Steven A. Harold

First edition published 2002
Reprinted 2003
Second edition 2005
Third edition 2008
Fourth edition 2011

British Library Cataloguing in Publication Data.
A catalogue record for this book is available from the British Library.

ISBN 978 1 84528 449 7

Cover design by Baseline Arts Ltd, Oxford
Produced for How To Books by Deer Park Productions, Tavistock
Typeset by Kestrel Data, Exeter, Devon
Printed and bound by Bell & Bain Ltd, Glasgow

NOTE: The material contained in this book is set out in good faith for general
guidance and no liability can be accepted for loss or expense incurred as a result of
relying in particular circumstances on statements made in the book. Laws and
regulations are complex and liable to change, and readers should check the
current position with the relevant authorities before making personal
arrangements.

Contents

In Memory of

Dr. David Allen Page
1942–2000

'*We are what we are
and we do what we do.*'

Acknowledgements

I would like to thank the many people who have played a part in bringing this book into existence. To Terence Watts for being my unofficial mentor in my early days of practice; Nicola Martin of the Institute of Clinical Hypnosis for providing the opportunity to change my dreams into reality; Pauline and Dennis Yates for being my editors; my parents Raymond and Mavourneen for always being there. Lastly, my special thanks must go to John for his encouragement, support and belief in me.

Preface

Today there are hundreds of alternative and complementary therapies available to the general public as well as the more conventional therapies of psychotherapy or counselling. The vast majority of these therapies are not available through your doctor. They have to be sought out. To benefit from these therapies the public has to find therapists who are in private practice.

As well as the existence of many different types of therapy, there are also hundreds of schools offering training on how to become a therapist in any chosen subject – from acupuncture to reiki, from kinesiology to naturopathy – there are many options with which to make your trade in the alternative and conventional medicine arena. You can take a correspondence course, a course over a period of years or an intensive course over a period of days and at the end call yourself a therapist. A course should not be judged by the period of time involved. Some of the best and most skilful therapists are self-taught and have never seen the inside of a classroom since leaving school.

Whichever way you become competent in your skill, you will have one major lesson to learn when you graduate: how to attract clients to your practice. Some schools do an excellent job of providing their graduates with the necessary business skills to enable them to taste success quickly. Others do not provide an adequate grounding or the type of continued support necessary to help a fledgling therapist move from seeing an occasional client to having a full-time practice. Many therapy graduates have expectations of becoming a full-time therapist. They may see an opportunity of moving from a career that bores them to something more exciting. Without appropriate marketing skills, they are likely to fail and will probably return to their old career or at best have a very part-time business in which they occasionally attract a client or two.

You should not jump from a full-time career to self-employment in one leap unless you have a safety net in place! The safety net could be a redundancy lump sum, a supportive partner or other funding to help you while you get your practice up and running. If you don't have any of these then you should consider reducing your hours in the old profession as you increase the hours in the new career. You could negotiate a reduction in the hours with your current employer such as moving from a five-day week to four days. As your therapy practice expands over a period of time, you can reduce the hours you spend in the old career, eventually making a complete career change. This approach brings the comfort of knowing you have another source of income and takes away some of the financial pressure from your therapy practice.

Being a successful therapist, particularly in private practice, requires good marketing skills. It is no good being the most effective therapist in the world if you don't tell the world that you exist. Your practice will be a success or failure depending on your therapy and marketing skills. Most therapists have to find out the hard way what works for them and what doesn't.

Some new therapists fall into the trap of attempting to 'buy' their clients, in effect throwing away their hard-earned funds (usually saved from their previous career) into advertising. Any form of promotion should be researched and approached in the same manner you would use with your therapy clients.

Advertising is not marketing but is just one part of the process. Marketing involves the four Ps: Product (or service), Promotion, Price and Place. Each has an important role to play. Get any one of them wrong and you will lose business. To the four Ps we should add a fifth P: Persistence. Persistence pays dividends.

The purpose of this book is to give you so many ways of marketing your practice that it will be virtually impossible to fail. Yet, even armed with this book some will still not see the light. A history teacher whose students were worried about a forthcoming exam was heard to say that even if she gave them all the questions, there would be some students who would still fail. Her message was simple: having the information to succeed is one thing, using it is another. If you want to succeed you need to take action again and again.

If you use this book as it is intended to be used you should be able to create a tidal wave of enquiries from potential clients. Take the ideas detailed here and not only use them as they stand but also adapt them to your circumstances. When you have undertaken all the marketing methods in this book you will be ready to start from the beginning again. There are many more than 101 ways to market your practice. You will know that you are successful when you start to create your own ideas.

Look at it this way: if you just manage to attract one extra client through reading this book, it will have paid for itself. In reality this book has the potential to pay for itself over and over again.

Acknowledging the Message v Medium

Before you get into the contents of this practical book on marketing, it is important to know about an aspect of marketing that will make or break your efforts.

All the tips in this book are very practical. The book's aim is to offer such a broad spectrum of ideas that any therapist who is based in or near any reasonably-sized town or city, should never be short of ideas on how to market their practice.

Yet some therapists, despite having these 101 client-attracting ideas, will still not enjoy enough business to survive financially as a therapist. Even if this book had 1001 ideas some therapists would still struggle to get enough fee-paying clients each and every week. There is a very good reason for this as you will soon discover.

The purpose of this chapter is to explain for example why a therapist in Leeds will fail and yet another therapist offering the same therapy and who is also based in Leeds will succeed.

Believe it or not, the difference between those two therapists will not be that one has a bigger marketing budget or is a more skilled therapist than the other, although these factors do make a difference of course. But that is not the reason for the difference in the success of their individual practices in this example.

REJECTING MARKETING IDEAS THAT DON'T WORK

As therapists and enlightened human beings, you will know that if you want something new to happen you need to do something new. A well-known and well-worn NLP phrase is 'if you keep doing the same old thing, you tend to end up with the same old result'. This is of course true.

The problem is that some therapists will 'throw the baby out with the bath water'. In other words they will discard something that looks ineffective, not realising that it has the potential to be effective. To elucidate: they may dismiss a marketing idea as 'not working' when in fact it may have the potential to be just what their business needs: a source for attracting clients.

Too often a therapist will hear from a colleague about how well a method of marketing has worked for them. Their colleague will state in glowing terms how many clients they have got through their campaign.

As an example, let's say that this successful marketing idea is a classified advert in a local newspaper.

Having heard that a classified advert worked so well for their colleague, our therapist will probably decide that they will do the same in their local newspaper. Unfortunately that is often where the similarity ends. The classified ad falls flat. It just doesn't deliver anything like the number of clients required to make the cost worthwhile.

Then a decision is made which goes something like this, 'classified ads do not work for my therapy' or 'tried that and it doesn't work for me'.

Now of course there is a possibility that the two comments above are accurate. However, the therapist who made them will never know for sure because they stopped doing any more classified advertising in that newspaper after just one or two attempts. Let's face it, if we stopped doing something after just a couple of attempts we probably would never have learnt to walk or ride a bike.

SHOOTING THE MESSENGER

Have you heard the expression 'Don't shoot the messenger' before? I am sure you have. It stems from ancient times when communications were delivered by a messenger and sometimes the messengers were put to the sword if the message content displeased the recipient.

Nowadays, if we have to inform someone of bad news and the reaction we get from the recipient is unpleasant we might say in our defence, 'Don't blame me, I was only asked to give you this message.'

So how does this apply to the previous classified advert example, you might ask? Well, the newspaper is the 'messenger' and the advert itself is the 'message' in this example.

The wording you use in the advert or the 'copy' as it is referred to in marketing circles, will make or break that advert's success.

The newspaper (or messenger) may offer the best and most cost-effective way of promoting your therapy service. It may have the highest potential to bring you numerous clients but, if you get your copy (or message) wrong, you will never know what you missed. You may mistakenly decide that classified adverts do not work for you, just like that therapist did.

Now a caveat is required here. No therapist, unless they have limitless funds, can afford to continually experiment with a marketing idea like classified adverts. Only the large corporations have the vast sums required to experiment with their marketing to the nth degree.

What this means is that you need to get your copy as perfect as possible the first time. However, if you think your first attempt at writing is going to be good enough, you probably need to think again.

Even the most talented copywriters will never be satisfied with the first copy they produce. They will keep refining and changing and playing with words until they are happy with every single word they have used. This is why you should always be as meticulous as possible with the words you use for any marketing medium. This includes your brochures, leaflets, websites and business cards too.

INTRODUCING THE ELEMENTS OF COPY

'Copy' refers to any words, sentences and descriptions you use to market your business. It can even include punctuation and any part of the written message. The term 'copy' applies to all your marketing media.

Depending on whether you are crafting a sales letter, website, leaflet, flyer or other marketing medium, typically, copy will consist of one or more of these elements:

1. **Pre-heading** – A sentence in a smaller size font than the headline that gives a lead into the heading.

2. **Heading or Headline** – this is what the eye will focus on first because it has the biggest font and is meant to stick out from the text around it. The headline does the job of acting as bait. It must intrigue the reader in 3 seconds or less or risk losing the reader. Often the 'problem' is stated here, for example, 'Finding Life A Struggle? Are You Always Feeling Stressed?'

3. **Sub-heading** – A sentence that supports the headline and contains more words than the headline and again encourages the reader to keep reading.

4. **Opening salutation** – things like 'Dear friend' or 'Hello, fellow entrepreneur' or other salutation if you can't address the reader by name. This is only used usually with a letter, ezine (a magazine sent via email) and sometimes a website.

5. **Body text** (words, sentences, paragraphs) – always err on the side of less words. Keep sentences short as they convey a sense of energy to the reader. Keep paragraphs short so that reading does not seem like hard work

6. **Body text sub-headings** – where possible give paragraphs a subheading to break up the text. Some readers will skim read by using these sub-headings.

7. **Questions** – ask questions when you can because it forces the reader to answer them mentally. A question should lead to an answer that makes the reader want to find out more. However,

don't overuse this as it will seem like an interrogation and turn the reader off.

8. **Slogans** – a well chosen slogan may well stick in the memory more easily than many other parts of your copy.

9. **Quotes** – enclosing sentences in quotation marks gives a sense of authority to that sentence. Such as 'Excess stress can lead to premature death'. Use quotations sparingly to retain their power. Interestingly, you can make up your quotations and they will still maintain an aura of authority and substance.

10. **Cases histories** – if you have the space, write about a client of yours who had a problem and how you helped them to overcome it. Unless you have your ex-client's permission to use their experience, change the details so that no one is able to recognise them from your description.

    The reader will often be convinced by this case history because they will see similarities between themselves and the person you describe.

11. **Bullet points** – a way of making what you want to communicate to the reader as easy to read as possible. Used in the right way bullet points can create an overwhelming sense of so many reasons to take up your offer.

    Use bullet points to summarise what you have already said. Repeating what you have said in another way helps memory and emphasises important points.

Use bullet points for emphasising the problem. With the stress example you could say:

Prolonged stress may lead to:

- physical ailments such as ulcers and IBS

- sleep disturbance and insomnia

- difficulty in personal relationships

- short temper

- premature death.

Likewise, use bullet points to highlight the positives of the service you offer, for example:

Regular meditation can lead to:

- a feeling of harmony and balance

- more restful sleep

- better relationships with partners, spouses, children

- feelings of calmness and control

- a longer and healthier life.

12. **Testimonials** – if you can include even one testimonial it really can make a big difference. The nearest thing to a personal recommendation for your service is to be able to publish a testimonial. Just make sure that you have the permission of the client to do this if you show their name.

13. **Guarantee** – this is useful for dealing with what is known as 'buyer's remorse'. It's the moment of doubt that a buyer of a service or product might have before and sometimes after a purchase. Before the purchase happens you can help prevent this by offering some form of assurance. This is not so easy as far as a therapy service is concerned because unlike with a product the customer cannot return something for a refund.

    Having said that, some 'stop smoking' therapists offer a guarantee. The guarantee is not necessarily about getting a refund, but is more likely to be the promise of having access to unlimited free sessions if the customer starts smoking again.

14. **Bonuses** – this is where you lay out anything extra you can offer. It adds extra value and attempts to convince the reader that they will miss a great opportunity if they don't take up your service.

An example might be offering a free 15-minute Indian head massage with every full massage session.

15. **Call to action** – this is often the aspect of the copy that the inexperienced will omit. A call to action tells the reader what to do. You will be amazed at how much we like to be led at times. By clearly stating the step that is needed you ensure that there is no confusion in the reader's mind.

Examples of a call to action are:

- To Reduce Your Stress Today Call 0800 0000 00 Now!
- Call Now To Book Your Massage Session!
- Phone Me Now Before All The Sessions Go!
- Contact Me Before August 30th To Get Your Discount!

16. **Closure** – this is how you sign off and close your copy. In a letter it would be something like 'Yours faithfully' or 'Yours sincerely'. Nowadays such old-fashioned forms of closure are no longer considered obligatory. Many people use closures such as 'Best wishes' or 'Warm regards' and other more informal word combinations.

In many instances when any marketing medium other than a letter is being written (an exception may be a website), this is not used.

17. **Post Scripts** – this is a great way of jogging the memory such as:

PS – Don't forget that this offer ends on 31 March 2010

In fact some people will use more than one postscript to quickly remind the reader of several benefits or what they will lose if they don't take up the offer.

18. **Pictures/Photographs/Images** – just as the song states 'a picture paints a thousand words'. Sometimes rather than trying to communicate a feeling or emotion an image can save you a lot of effort and convey more than words could do.

    Also an image breaks up any text and the idea is to encourage a potential customer to read your message and not to be turned off by a feeling that all those words look like too much hard work.

    Even though one image can say it all, sometimes you might want to direct the reader's imagination by giving the image a caption. A caption is simply four to six words immediately under the image. If you need ideas look at newspaper or magazine images and captions.

Those are the main elements of copy that you can use or need. Do remember it is never about using all of them.

As with anything that you want to communicate, think about a start, a middle and an ending.

ORDERING WHAT YOU WRITE ABOUT

The previous section of this chapter has given you a list and maybe a framework of elements that go to make up copy.

The next challenge is knowing the most effective words to use for any of those individual elements of headline, body text and so on.

State The Problem First

When any potential customer glances at your website, leaflet, flyer, brochure, advert or anything you employ to market your business, they will want to know that you understand their issue or problem.

You need to acknowledge their ailment and their pain and discomfort, whether that is physical, emotional or psychological.

The previous example of a headline repeated below was:

Finding Life A Struggle?
Are You Always Feeling Stressed?

Now this headline is also in the form of a question. When anyone reads these questions the answer will be 'yes' or 'no'. If the answer is 'no' then they probably won't read on and that is okay because you want to help people who are stressed.

The likelihood is that most people will answer 'yes'. In doing so, they will naturally feel you are talking to them (the word 'you' is included in the headline for this reason) and will want to find out more. The headline acts as an attention grabber and then leads them into wanting to read more.

Reading the AIDA principles on page 81 in the chapter entitled 'Advertising Plus!' in this book will help you further.

'What's In It For Me?'

All potential customers want to know that you have something to offer them. When they read your copy they will be mentally asking themselves 'What is in it for me?' If you know that they are looking for what they will gain by buying your service, this will give you a vital clue about the order of what to tell them in your marketing.

Now with this in mind you can deduce that they are looking to find out how they will benefit from your therapy. So describe the benefits of what you offer first. Use bullet points to create energy and excitement and momentum if need be.

By doing this you are tapping into their emotions. As humans we tend to make an emotional decision first and then look for a logical reason to support that decision.

The error that is easily made in marketing is talking about features before benefits. Think of benefits as what they will gain as a result of having your therapy. Think of features as the method, which includes the therapy, any equipment, environment and any other ways you use

9

to provide the ability to give them those benefits: An electric massage couch is a feature. A feeling of total relaxation is a benefit.

A massage client wants to know that they will feel relaxed (a benefit) before they will want to know how this will happen by massaging the body (a feature).

An example of a headline that uses a benefit is :

Soothe Your Aching Muscles in 30 minutes

An example of a headline that uses a feature is:

Enjoy A 30-Minute Massage

Desire, which is an emotion, is triggered in the headline that includes a benefit. However the second headline that uses a feature (massage) seems quite cold and uninviting.

Remember to state the benefits first and features second.

RECOGNISING THAT LESS CAN BE MORE

Most people have a natural tendency to err on the side of more detail rather than less. The logical thinking behind this is that that last extra bit of detail might just be enough to sway an interested reader to become a potential client.

While this can be accurate, if you include too much detail all those words will appear like hard work. They, the reader, may not go beyond your wonderful headline because they can see this huge body of text and it seems like too much work to wade through it all.

Leaving blank lines and including lots of space around small blocks of text makes the medium you are using a lot easier to read.

Simply put, marketing is about grabbing someone's attention, keeping their interest, increasing their desire and then getting them to buy from you.

If you can do that in 75 words rather than 100 so much the better!

BRINGING IT ALL TOGETHER

The aspects described above of designing any marketing medium may seem overwhelming when you first read through them. Here is a way of keeping matters simple and doable.

You need to bear in mind the marketing medium you intend to make a design for. If you are creating a telephone directory display ad, for example, you will have much less space compared to a website or practice brochure.

Also you need to consider what issue or issues you want to highlight in this particular campaign and the audience you want to aim for.

For example:
Issue = Sports injuries, muscle strains
Audience = Sportsmen and Women

Designing Your Copy

Use this method as a guide to creating your copy.

Start off with two blank sheets of paper. You can do this using word processing software on your computer or with a pen and paper.

Label the first sheet of paper or document: Resources. Label the second sheet of paper or document: Copy Draft.

Resources Sheet

Divide your resources sheet into roughly three sections.

In the first section put the subheading, *Problems*. The second section should be labelled *Benefits* and for the third section the subheading should be *Features*.

Now go ahead and write under each section, anything and everything you can think of to do with the focus of your marketing campaign.

Using the previous example your *Resources* document might resemble this:

You will use your *Resources* sheet to give you ideas of what to write about in sub-sections on your *Copy Draft* document.

Resources

Problem(s):
Muscle Strain, Aches, Pains, Injury

Benefit(s):
Eases pain, helps healing, soothes muscle strain, promotes better sleep, quicker injury recovery, prevents old injury repetition, get back to playing your sport more quickly, feel better, optimistic, improved concentration, reduced risk of future injuries, more confidence

Feature(s):
Sports massage, hot stone massage, confidential, aromatherpy, experienced therapist, qualified, past successes, comfortable couch, a full hour of therapy, free consultation, specialised sports injury massage, professional

The *Copy Draft* document will include a number of, but not necessarily all, the elements of copy design mentioned earlier in this chapter ranging from the Pre-heading through to Postscripts.

Remember this is a first draft and not the final copy. Do not expect to get it right the first time.

If you are designing a telephone directory display advert you will probably be limited to four or five elements of copy. Your *Copy Draft* might start off like this:

HEADING – this is the problem(s)

Sub-heading – want to be free of problem?

Body text – benefits

Body text features

Call to Action

Postscript

Then as you develop it a possible version might look like this:

Fed Up With Muscle Strain
or Injury After Sport?

Want to recover more quickly and prevent injuries?

Imagine your aches soothed away, your injury
healing faster and you feeling more confident!

Specialised Sports Injury Massage
Charles Bloggs MTH
Experienced and Professional Massage Therapist

Call 0800 000 000 Now
Don't Let Sports Injuries Ruin Your Game!

Notice how the *Resources* sheet has provided the clues to completing this advert, also that only four or five of the total number of copy elements have been used. This advert is by no means finished as it can be refined further by playing with words and font sizes.

A suggestion is that you end up with four or five different advert designs. Sometimes the difference between one design and another can just be one word in the heading.

When you have four or five designs, print them out on paper and compare them in pairs. Comparing in pairs will make it easier to decide which advert appeals to you most. It can also be a good idea to show these designs to friends or colleagues to get their opinions.

REFINING YOUR COPY FURTHER

By now you will have realised that drafting copy is an art and skill. It is something that anyone can learn how to do and do well. Like any form of art and skill you can refine and improve on what you produce.

A great and easy way of increasing your ability to write great copy is to be more observant when reading a magazine or newspaper. Pay attention to the advertising and analyse why one advert works and another one leaves you cold. Doing this will improve your copywriting skills in leaps and bounds.

Even television adverts can be a lesson in themselves. There is a well-known clothes and food retailer who is particularly adept at promoting their goods and particularly their food.

For example if you were going to describe one of their products such as a roast dinner, you might just say:

'Get our roast beef dinner with potatoes, carrots and gravy.'

That sentence above says exactly what the product is; however it is not very exciting and the imagination of the customer is not encouraged.

However this particular retailer typically promotes the same food item by saying:

'Experience the taste of our tender Scottish roast beef, served with lightly-salted golden Jersey potatoes, honey drizzled organic carrots and covered with our thick onion gravy.'

This second description gets the imagination involved and indeed may even have the hypnotic effect of creating saliva in the mouth.

Here is a copywriting lesson for free. Use words that bring out the feelings that paint a vivid mental picture of what your customer can expect to experience with your therapy. The better the picture you paint, the more you engage your customer's imagination and the more they will want to see you and not your competition.

A famous US theme park's ethos supports this idea. They are not selling high-speed or themed fairground rides. Their customers are buying an experience. An experience they will talk about and encourage others to experience also.

Whether it's shoes, fairground rides, food or therapy, your marketing goal should be the same: Let your customers buy an experience from you. The challenge for you is how to communicate that experience in your copy.

Get it right and you will be that therapist who is always booked up weeks in advance.

ACKNOWLEDGING THE MESSAGE v MEDIUM

Increase the return on your marketing investment by using descriptions that fire your customer's imagination within a tried and tested design structure for your copy.

Choosing Practice Places

Even the part-time or occasional therapist needs a place to practise from. One of the most important considerations is where this will be. Factors such as cost, availability, facilities, environment and location play a critical part in getting it right.

The location in which you decide to practise your therapy can enhance or detract from your ability to attract clients. Fortunately there are a number of options available to choose from.

A great way of helping you make the right decision is to write down all the aspects that are important to you. Grading these aspects in order of importance helps you to identify those that are essential and those that you can be more flexible about.

1

WORKING FROM HOME

Many therapists start a practice from their home. The home provides a number of advantages for the new or experienced therapist as long as you live in a convenient location for your clients. There are also disadvantages.

Advantages

- No extra rental costs are involved for the use of a room at home.

- There are no long-term contract commitments.

- The home offers a degree of anonymity to your client.

- It's more comfortable and relaxed in your own home.

- There's more flexibility about when you see your clients.

- No time is lost travelling and there are no transport costs.

Disadvantages

- Possible disruption to your family.

- Clients may query your professionalism.

- Maintaining parts of your home to clinical standards.

- Inconvenience of having a room that may have to be rearranged every day between family and therapy use.

- You may not be able to offer a separate waiting room.

Your local council will not usually have any objections to you running a therapy business from home as long as the external appearance of your residence is not altered and the running of the business does not upset neighbours. A mortgage lender may want you to take out a different insurance policy if they become aware that you work from home.

Essential home preparations

From the first moment a new client sees your home they are going to be judging you. They will be looking at your privet hedge or the lawn of your front garden. If these are neat and tidy, the client will start to piece together a favourable impression of your home and you. If the garden is a complete eyesore, they will start to have second thoughts. Once someone starts to formulate an opinion they look for more evidence to support that opinion. If they then spot yellowish net curtains and a window that has been patched up with cardboard, don't expect them to come back!

We are all guilty of getting used to how our home looks, good or bad. We have seen that bare patch of wall so many times that our mind no longer registers its significance. A great way of finding out how your property is viewed through the eyes of a client is to get a friend to pretend to be a client. Get them to approach your home as though they were seeing it for the first time. Encourage them to be honest. Once you have a list of areas that could be improved, it is down to you whether to change them or not.

The survey by your friend should continue past the front door and you should greet them like a prospective client. Guide them all the way through the hallway into your treatment room and talk to them as though they have arrived for their first therapy session. Your friend should not only keep their eyes peeled for matters that are not so pleasant but also utilise the other four senses: smell, taste, hearing and touch.

The treatment room

Not everyone will have the luxury of owning a room whose sole purpose will be for therapy. From a tax (capital gains) perspective it is better if the room has a dual purpose. You may have to opt to use one of the busiest rooms in the house, such as the living room. This will restrict members of the family to certain areas of the home when you are treating a client. Your family will have to be discreet, curtail some of their usual activities and keep noise to a minimum. Doors to other rooms will need to be closed for privacy and your family will need to avoid meeting your client in the hallway or on the way to the toilet. Also be aware of any cooking odours.

Clients will probably be happy about seeing personal items in a room because this helps them to formulate an idea of your personality and interests. If you have a client seeking help with problems in their family, they will feel that you are likely to be more empathetic if they see a family photograph in the room. Alternatively, this might work against you if your client is single and has a perception that you do not view the world as they do. These indications of your personal life can be helpful, unhelpful or neutral, so look around your room and imagine how your clients will react to it.

You may have to go to the inconvenience of constantly rearranging the practice room for your first client and then when you are finished for the day having to put the room back to its original order. You will need to consider where will you store therapy items (couches, towels, oils, electronic equipment, etc.) between practice times and you will require a secure filing system for your client records. Your clients will want to be assured that their details will remain confidential. If you maintain client records you will need to comply with the Data Protection Act (details of the regulations can be found at your local library).

If you are unable to use a room on the ground floor then you have the concern that a particular client may have great difficulty negotiating stairs. A ground floor treatment room and upstairs toilet presents a similar problem.

Building rapport

Build rapport quickly. Your client is coming to a strange building (your home) to meet a person they have only ever spoken to on the telephone. The first few moments of meeting someone are very significant if the relationship is going to work.

When they knock at the door, unless you have a receptionist, it should be you, the therapist who greets them. Do not send one of your children to answer the door as your professional status will plummet.

Your first words should be precise, clear and yet friendly. Repeat the client's name and introduce yourself with a firm handshake. For example, 'Hello, David, my name is Susan Blake. I am the kinesiologist.' In the space of a few seconds you have achieved a number of important things. You have confirmed to the client that they were expected and have come to the right address. You have confirmed your name and that you are the therapist. You have assured them that you are in control. Clients want to feel that you know what you are doing. This positive welcome gets you off to a great start.

When they get to the treatment room make sure that they have time to have a good look around before you close the door to the room. Do not be in any hurry to shut them in. Building rapport varies from person to person and therapy to therapy. Some practitioners will offer the client a cup of coffee or tea or a glass of water at this point. If they accept, from a psychological point of view it can be quite significant. It shows they are willing to accept something from you and this can also help them to relax more in your company. The subconscious mind will remember an association between tea or coffee and a nice comfortable chat with friends or family.

Some therapists do not offer refreshments but prefer to keep matters on a business-like level. There are pros and cons with either approach. You should decide which one you are happy with. Of course the drink may delay matters or may not be appropriate prior to the therapy you offer. Time may also be a factor. If you have to wait 15 minutes for your client to finish their herbal tea before you can massage them, your next session will be delayed.

Safety at home

There are security risks posed by having a stranger in your home: risks to your personal safety and to your property.

If you have other family members in the home when clients call then you will feel a lot safer. All new clients are strangers until you get to know them and form that professional relationship. Your clients will want to feel safe and secure with you and the building they are visiting for treatment. If they know or sense that they are not alone with you in the home, they will generally feel safer and more relaxed. This is particularly true of a male therapist and female client and vice versa, but not exclusively.

Keep a mobile telephone handy with a telephone number pre-programmed. This can be a useful way of letting a relative, friend or neighbour know you need help. After some experience most therapists are able to tell from the first telephone call whether they should agree to see a new client or not. If you are not sure and do agree to see a client it would be wise to let someone know that you may need their intervention. Knowing you have this arrangement can help you to relax more. There is nothing worse than the therapist being more nervous than the client!

Working from home can be just as successful as from a clinic as long as you have taken into account all the factors involved.

2

WORKING FROM A THERAPY CENTRE

For many reasons you may decide that to practise from home is not appropriate. You may conclude that it would be best to work some days from home and others from a therapy centre or clinic. For the therapist, this is a popular option.

Advantages

■ You'll have a room specifically for therapy.

■ There is no inconvenience to your family.

■ There is a receptionist to take your bookings.

■ There is a waiting room for clients who arrive early.

■ Clients may be able to pay for treatment using credit cards.

■ Networking with other therapists working there will reduce your feeling of isolation.

■ Working at the clinic gives a greater sense of professionalism.

■ You may receive referrals from other fellow therapists who use the centre.

■ You can share advertising costs.

■ Personal safety may be improved.

■ It will be a quiet environment.

Disadvantages

■ There are extra costs involved in paying for the room.

■ You can only see clients when the room is available.

■ There will be travelling time to the therapy centre and transport costs.

■ The environment may be too clinical and stark for the client.

■ The clinic's location on a busy high street may reduce anonymity.

Deciding where to practise

To help you decide whether a particular therapy centre is appropriate, take a friend or relative with you when you visit for the first time to act as an extra pair of eyes. It is amazing what you, the therapist, can overlook when getting caught up in the excitement of visualising yourself in full practice. A level-headed friend can point this out to you.

Take into account accessibility for certain types of clients. Not all clients will have their own means of transport and may rely on trains or buses to get about. Check how frequently these run and how close these facilities are to your intended practice. Find out about the train and bus timetables because your clients will expect you to have this information and you will want to make it easy for them to see you. Also locate where the nearest car parks or restriction-free streets are. Poor transport communications can hamper the growth of your practice. You also need to check that the building has adequate facilities for a person with a disability.

Generally, a room in a therapy health centre will come ready for your immediate use. You pay for a room that is pleasant, clean and fresh. The adjacent rooms will be used by other therapists who respect the need for confidentiality and control of noise.

You won't have to concern yourself with family members trudging around the house or the sound of stereos, televisions or radios being too loud. There will be no pets to control or cooking smells to mask. Access for people with a disability should also be better.

Usually, the clinic will have a central reception and waiting area, all adding to the air of professionalism. The receptionist will take bookings for you and greet your clients when they arrive for their appointments to see you. The clinic will have (by law) a suitable number of toilets that will be cleaned and freshened on a regular basis. Some clinics also provide showers for clients.

Good clinics also consider the smaller touches which make a real difference. They may provide boxes of tissues in each room, fresh flowers, water coolers and coffee- and tea-making facilities. The receptionist may even offer to make coffee or tea for your client before the appointment starts. All these extras add an air of welcome to your clients and will help with word-of-mouth marketing.

Costs and payments

The clinic may offer an arrangement for the client to pay the clinic directly. You will be reimbursed your client fees (less the room rent) at the end of the week. This can be useful when your client wants to pay by credit card. It is far more economical and logical for the clinic to deal with credit card transactions rather than an individual therapist.

You will be expected to hire a room in blocks of four or five hours each week. Whether you have clients during all, part of or none of these hours, you will still be charged for the room. The best times are from five o'clock in the evening on weekdays. This is the time that most people will have finished work and be available for therapy. Saturdays are also popular with clients for the same reason.

If you are unable to secure these times then think twice about operating from that clinic or negotiate a better deal for the less popular times. You may even be able to persuade the clinic to give you floating times that you use on an hour-by-hour basis and pay for only when you have a client.

The treatment room

No room is ever ideal and so you will need to be able to see the potential. You can add to a room's feel and ambience but you should not have to bring in large items of furniture. You can add a cushion, pillow or throw if you want to add to the cosiness or you may decide that simple and clinical is better. Either way, you can completely change the feel of a place by using your creativity and moving furniture around or adding little extras. You need to be as comfortable in your surroundings as your client is going to be.

You can enhance the room by adding some personal touch of your own. This can be something as simple as a favourite essential oil in an oil burner or fresh flowers.

Building rapport

When your new client comes for their first appointment this is most likely the first time that they will have had any contact with you. They will generally only have had contact with the receptionist and so will only know your name and some of your details. If you practise from home, you will have spoken to the new client on the telephone and the important factor of building a working relationship will already have begun.

It's said first impressions count, so here is your chance to make or break the relationship in the first minutes. Consciously or subconsciously, you are being assessed by your client from the very first point of contact. So be confident, be focused and know what you are doing. Make some 'small talk' with the client as you guide them to the treatment room.

Once the client is in the room be concerned about their comfort and give an outline of the immediate session. If this is an assessment session, tell them this again and the choices that they will have at the end of it. The more you keep your client informed, the more comfortable they will feel, and nothing will surprise them.

Safety at the clinic

Your own safety should be enhanced at a clinic for the simple reason that there are always people coming and going. Even if you are the only therapist working in the evening, there should always be another person in the building such as the receptionist or the person responsible for closing up at night.

Fellow therapists

You will gradually meet the other therapists working at the clinic. This is a great opportunity for gaining referrals and exchanging therapies. Working at the centre can help to reduce the isolation often felt by people who have changed from an employed status and working with others, to self-employed and working alone. The cost of advertising can also be shared among the therapists and the therapy centre.

3

RENTING A ROOM

Practising from a rented room in a building that is not a 'designated' clinic or therapy centre has the potential to be as successful as any other option. Many aspects are similar to renting a room in a clinic. However, there are other issues that need to be taken into account.

Advantages

- Rental costs (pro rata) are significantly less than in a therapy centre or clinic.
- You'll have sole use of the room.
- There are more options with regard to the location of your practice.
- You will enjoy networking opportunities with neighbouring businesses.

Disadvantages

- You will incur costs of bringing the room to an acceptable standard.

- There is lack of control over noise from neighbouring businesses.

- The building may lack reception facilities.

- You will need to take into account travelling time to the building and transport costs.

Surveying the room and building

Assuming you are renting the room for a minimum of six months and that you are the only user of the room, you may get a completely empty room, in which case you can furnish it exactly the way you want. Usually you will not find any objection from the owners if you want to improve the decoration of the room. It can be quite a bonus to have a blank canvas and be able to create a room with your own personal touches.

Unfortunately, there is a possibility that this room may have neighbours whose businesses can be noisy or, through the nature of their business reflect badly on you. It is imperative that you find out who your neighbours are. You will not want to achieve complete silence but will need a room that is not going to be disturbed by excessive noise, smells or other environmental factors.

As the sole occupant of the room you will be responsible for keeping it in a usable and acceptable condition to your clients. Therefore you will need to clean and maintain the facilities within the room. The hallway leading to the rooms will generally be the responsibility of the building management and you should be aware of their arrangements regarding the maintenance of this area.

You may also find it necessary to provide refreshments for your clients such as water from a dispenser or hot drinks. The provision of this and other minor details is down to your own personal taste. It is worth noting that paying attention to small details like this can really make a difference to how your clients feel about the quality of service you provide.

The building may still have a receptionist or security guard but they will not be as welcoming as a receptionist in a clinic. You may wish to make an arrangement with the receptionist that your clients are either directed to your room or asked to wait in the reception area for you to meet and greet them. Trial and error will, as always, teach you the best way to operate.

Once you have committed yourself to renting or leasing a room in a multi-purpose building it is a good idea to get to know your neighbours. Make friends with them and they will be more likely to co-operate should you need to ask for anything. This is an opportunity to network and you may be surprised how many clients are referred to you from the businesses in the same building if you take the trouble to build good relationships with them.

4

PROVIDING MOBILE THERAPY

The more options you can offer a client, the more you are likely to satisfy their needs and circumvent any objections. Objections are reasons that potential customers have for not making a buying decision. Offering a mobile form of your therapy can be a way of reaching those clients who for various reasons cannot get to you. These might be mothers who cannot leave their home because of their children; they could be older people who have no transport and cannot negotiate public transport; it could be someone who suffers from a phobia about cars, tubes and trains or even agoraphobia (fear of open spaces).

Advantages

- There are no rental costs.
- There is no disruption to the family home.

27

- You will not have any lease or rent contract commitments.

- The client will be more relaxed in their own home.

Disadvantages

- You will be practising in a strange environment.

- There will be the uncertainty of available facilities.

- You will incur extra transport costs and lose time travelling to and from appointments.

- You will have to transport your therapy equipment.

Structuring your fees

As a mobile therapist, what you save on room rent costs, you lose on transport costs and your time in travelling to the client's home. All these factors should be taken into account when deciding your fee structure. People are willing to pay a higher price for the convenience of having the service come to them. Include an additional amount for the travelling time and costs in your therapy fees.

Many newly-qualified therapists, who initially have no place from which to practise, start off their business by visiting clients in their homes. Once they are established they tend to drop the mobile option from their service, yet it can be a useful extra, particularly if no-one else is offering it.

Taking control of your practice

The drawback of offering a mobile service is that you are not in as much control as you would like to be. You are reliant on your client being able to provide some of the facilities needed for your therapy – aspects like a quiet and private room, a comfortable armchair and wash facilities. There may be an occasion when your client is not at home when you arrive for the appointment. There is nothing more annoying than travelling to see someone who is not in when you arrive.

Given enough thought, many of these situations can be eased or avoided altogether. Emphasise with any client the minimum facilities that you must have at their home. You might ask them to pay for their session in advance to cover the possibility of them not keeping the appointment.

Mobile therapy can work very well for any therapist as long as you consider all the different dimensions of operating this way.

5

BUYING AN EXISTING PRACTICE

Just like any other commercial concern, you can get the opportunity to buy another person's practice. The word 'practice' can mean many things. It could mean the whole building, existing clients (private and corporate) and past clients and any current employees plus ongoing arrangements and agreements (including advertising). It could also simply mean the existing clients. It is not the purpose of this chapter to go into all the intricacies of purchasing an existing business but to point out some of the advantages and disadvantages. You should always seek professional advice on any major purchase of this nature.

Advantages

- You will have an immediate client base.

- You are taking over an established business.

- Set procedures and systems will be in place.

- Goodwill can help you to get off to a flying start.

Disdavantages

- You will have the initial purchase expense.

■ Existing clients may change to another therapist.

If everything goes well, purchasing an existing practice means that you are up and running immediately. With goodwill included, the vendor should have made clear the strategies that work for this practice, so you have systems and procedures in place and an existing client base. If the business has been successful and you repeat those past strategies, then logically you should be able to continue that success. One of the biggest assets should be that the practice is well known because it has been in business for some time.

On the other hand, how successful is the practice really?

■ Why is the person selling the business?

■ Will all the clients be happy to see a new therapist or will they take this opportunity to stop their therapy or seek out a different therapist?

■ Will past clients object to you contacting them?

■ If the practice is known by the (selling) therapist's name, will you be able to trade using that name even though they no longer work at the practice?

As long as you have weighed up all these considerations, then there is no reason why purchasing an existing practice at the right price cannot be a success and get you over the hurdles of starting a brand new practice.

6

SETTING UP IN SPORTS CENTRES

Major sports centres provide additional services often under the umbrella of the 'Beauty and Health Suite'. These regular services can be facials, manicures and pedicures and hair styling. The facilities in these suites may be appropriate for your type of therapy.

Very few health suites will be fully booked throughout the week. The management of the suite will be interested in offering other complementary services to the public to fill those empty slots. If you can offer a service which is not currently being provided and the facilities they have (massage couch, private cubicle, washing facilities, etc.) are appropriate for your therapy, you may find an additional place to ply your trade.

A convenient arrangement is to agree a set time and day that you would see your clients at the centre. The centre will normally take responsibility for attracting clients and giving them appointment times. Their general marketing programme can now include the service you offer. The responsibility for getting clients would be the centre's and not yours. For this reason it is important to obtain an understanding that you only pay for rental of the space or room when you have a client booked. If you don't have a client then you don't pay for the time and the room can be used by another therapist.

The usefulness of this idea is that you do not have to concern yourself with marketing your services because the centre will have its own blanket advertising strategy. Successful therapists assist this by providing leaflets and posters.

7

SERVICING PRIVATE HEALTH CLUBS

In an effort to attract as many clients as possible, private health clubs and health farms are offering as many therapies as possible. In the old days it used to be a gym, with a fitness regime, maybe a diet to follow and a sauna and steam room. Today, any process or service that can enhance a customer's feel-good factor will be added to the range on offer. The larger the range of services, the more likely that a customer is going to find what they like and what works for them.

Complementary and alternative therapies are being added to many health resorts' menus. A massage service has nearly always been available but now you can get aromatherapy, osteopathy, Alexander

Technique, yoga and much more. With this in mind, you can form an agreement with these places and enjoy a steady flow of clients.

Some health clubs will take responsibility for marketing your therapy and book in clients for you on a set day and at a set time. Others will take more of a back seat and expect you to provide leaflets and posters and make yourself available to promote your service.

Costs to therapists vary. Some places will charge rent for a room and others will take a percentage of your fee. Make sure you know in advance which system is going to operate as you may need to increase your usual fees. Generally, you will be allocated a set number of hours on an agreed day each week. This makes matters easier, as knowing when you will offer your therapy at the club will enable you to arrange your private clients at other times.

Your initial approach to health clubs or resorts is best done by telephone. There is no point in writing a letter to a place that doesn't have the room or has someone else offering your therapy already. Phoning also gives you the opportunity to find out the name of the person to contact. You might be invited to have a look around immediately, but, if not, follow up your telephone call with a letter. Include the benefits of your therapy to their clients and how well it has been received in other places (if you can, give examples). State the bare minimum of facilities you would require. After a week follow the letter up with another telephone call to the named contact while the matter is still fresh in their mind. You can approach a private gymnasium in a similar way.

8

WORKING AS A CORPORATE ON-SITE THERAPIST

Large corporations have many facilities which are often under-utilised. Instead of offering a group workshop or course to a large company you could try offering to be an 'on-site' therapist. This type of employee benefit is becoming more and more popular.

Advantages

- There are no marketing costs.

- The company informs all employees about your services.

- There is the possible provision of a room without costs.

- Your reputation can spread like wild fire, particularly in an office or factory environment.

- Employees may also want to see you at your own private practice.

- Clients may recommend your therapy to friends, relatives and acquaintances.

Disadvantages

- Clients may not feel so comfortable seeking treatment while at work.

- Clients may be concerned about confidentiality.

Generally, the company provides private rooms and the necessary equipment in the room and then invites therapists to provide services such as autogenic training, homeopathy, reflexology and Indian head massage to name a few. Under the rules of the benefit, the employees may either make a contribution towards the service or the company may pay all the individual fees. Usually, the company just provides the facilities and the employee pays for the therapy that they undergo.

The benefits for the therapist are that you have a captive audience. You will have no marketing costs, as the company informs all employees that the service exists. You normally won't have any rent costs because the company provides the rooms. Your reputation can spread through word-of-mouth recommendations. You may also get employees preferring to see you in your own private practice away from prying eyes.

9

SETTING UP IN DOCTORS' SURGERIES

A great place to base your practice, even if it is only part time, is at a doctors' surgery. Many surgeries have spare rooms and it is a way for them to gain extra funds. Not all doctors will agree to this. It really comes down to how informed your local doctor is and their opinion on your therapy.

Advantages

■ You will receive referrals from the GPs in the practice.

■ There is an increased public perception of quality and professionalism.

■ Your therapy moves closer to being more widely accepted by the orthodox medical profession.

■ You will have reduced marketing costs.

Disadvantages

■ You will incur the extra costs involved in paying for the room.

■ You can only see clients within the surgery opening times.

■ You will have to take into account travelling time to the surgery and transport costs.

■ The environment may be too clinical and stark for the client.

■ The surgery management may restrict the ailments you can treat.

More and more therapists are securing rooms at surgeries. It is a great way to build a bridge between conventional and complementary medicine. In building better relations and because of the close proximity, you will start to receive referrals from the doctors who practise there. These will mostly be private patients but they will be referrals, none the less.

In the waiting area you will have a captive audience and practice managers will be more receptive to you leaving your leaflets in this area. Some therapists who secure a place at a doctor's surgery find that they can really cut down on their other marketing strategies.

Whether you practise full or part time from a doctor's surgery it will add an important dimension to your service: quality. Clients will assume that you must be good in order to be able to base yourself there. Perceptions count for a lot in any business.

CHOOSING PRACTICE PLACES

Many successful therapists have a portfolio of places to practise from. They may spend a different day of the week at different venues in different towns and cities.

Managing Your Practice

Every business or organisation needs to have a structured approach to handling the interaction between customers and the business. This is often referred to as CRM – Customer Relationship Management. Although most of it is common sense, this chapter will help you shape your customer service policy no matter how informal.

Pay attention to the small details of running a practice and you increase your chances of growing and maintaining a smooth and professional operation.

Never become complacent in your work, appearance or attitude or your practice will become shoddy, second-rate and this will be evident to your clients. You may lose them if this happens.

10

DECIDING WHAT TO CHARGE

Many new therapists stumble over how much to charge clients. The answer is to charge what you are worth. If you value what you provide, the client will value it too.

Deciding your value

Telephone the competition in your area to find out what their fees are for the service they provide. It is important to find out this information from a therapist who provides the same therapy as you. You need to compare like with like.

You will get a mix of prices and services. One therapist may charge £45 for an hour's therapy and give a free 15-minute consultation. Another will charge £75 for the first session, give a free 30-minute consultation, and then charge £55 for subsequent sessions. The idea of doing a survey of the competition is to gauge the range of fees that are appropriate to your location and therapy.

You do not have to keep within the range of fees you discover from your research, it is merely for you to make an informed decision about where to set your fees. The cost of therapy is a big part of the decision-making process for any potential client. Set your fees too low and they will think that your service lacks quality, that you don't have much experience or you are desperate for their business. You may start to begrudge the time you give your client and this is not a resourceful state to be in. Set your fees too high and you will be outside many clients' affordability range. It is far better to find a fee that respects your value, is affordable to the majority of enquirers and has taken into account your expenses. Remember that your expenses might include:

- heat
- light
- rent
- travel
- products
- equipment
- insurance
- professional fees.

Concessions

Some therapists offer a sliding scale of fees and a reduced fee to those who are unemployed, on low incomes or, for acceptable reasons, are unable to afford your full fee. Others believe that they should not reduce their fees. Indeed some would say that clients who are not punctual, do not carry out agreed tasks between sessions, or who simply do not keep their appointments often seem to be those who have been granted a reduced fee. It could be argued that a reduced fee brings with it a perception of lower value and a lack of motivation from the client.

If you give a reduction in your fees get the client to agree to see you during less popular times during the day. Prime times such as evenings and weekends should be the preserve of those who will pay your full fee.

Your practice rules

Clearly explain your practice rules to your clients. If you require 24 hours' notice of a cancellation, tell them. Let them know in advance what will be the forfeit if they do not follow this rule. If they give you less than 24 hours' notice the charge will be 50% of your fee, for example. Less than 12 hours' notice and the full fee will be due.

If you accept telephone bookings you can state your fees and cancellation policy and follow this up in writing as a way of confirming the appointment. Some therapists charge for one session in advance. This encourages the client to attend the appointment or to give you adequate notice that they can't make the time and date.

Your fee structure and rules of business should be made known to your client as soon as possible and then the chance of misunderstandings occurring will be reduced.

Lastly, you should review your fees at least annually to take into account changing circumstances and inflation.

11

MAKING IT EASY TO BUY

It would be a pity if, having attended many different therapy courses, read numerous therapy books, undergone examinations and joined appropriate associations, you fell at the final hurdle. Once a customer has made a decision to buy your service, you should make it as easy as possible for them to achieve that purchase.

Opening hours

Are your hours flexible enough for your clients? You will lose a potential client if you cannot find a convenient time. Most people will have a daytime occupation and will not be able to accept a daytime appointment. Your evening appointments will be very popular and at times these may be booked two or three weeks ahead, even though you still have plenty of daytime slots left.

If this pattern continues you may lose people who want to see you in a reasonable amount of time but are unable to because the nearest appointment you can give them is a month away. You should then consider whether to be available for some hours at the weekend. Many therapists have a Saturday morning clinic that takes the pressure off their evening times. Other therapists pick one day in the week when they will not see clients and then make themselves available for the whole of Saturday. The appointment times on Saturday should be the preserve of those who cannot make any other time. Use it as a fall back position only if you are unable to agree a convenient appointment time during the weekdays with a client.

At the commencement of any new practice you may need to accept bookings at odd and often inconvenient times. When you get busier, you can start to be more selective about the hours that you make yourself available.

Payment

The client has had their therapy session and now the time has come for them to pay your fee. The easiest payment method for the therapist is cash. After that the next easiest payment method is a cheque with a banker's guarantee card. How will you handle the situation if the client is expecting to be able to pay by credit card? If you can't accept credit cards and the client does not have enough cash or a cheque book with them, what will you do?

To avoid the above embarrassing situation you have two options. You can either tell the client in advance that you can't accept credit card payments (and risk the loss of business) or you can take steps to arrange to accept credit cards. The cost of accepting payment this way will be a percentage of your fee to the credit card company. Some companies require you to make a payment for any equipment needed to process a credit card transaction. New therapists can operate quite successfully without accepting credit card payments. As you become busier and your fee increases you may find that a credit card facility is a necessity. In fact some clients may not take you seriously if you don't accept credit cards.

Location

If you are not sure of how to get to your practice from other locations, how do you expect your clients to arrive there on time? Acquaint yourself with all the forms of transport that can help someone to find your practice easily and effortlessly. Memorise bus numbers and train timetables. Familiarise yourself with different routes so that you can give directions to anyone travelling by car. Go over the directions you give out and make them as 'idiot proof' as you can.

If at all possible try to send directions by email, fax or letter. The more you assist your client's journey the greater their chances of arriving on time, and in a good state of mind. Just try having a therapy session with someone who is 30 minutes late and flustered – and you can only give them 45 minutes because of your next appointment. Help your clients and you will help your practice to run smoothly.

12

CONVERTING ENQUIRIES INTO CLIENTS

Getting the client to telephone, write to or email you is the first step in the marketing process. The subsequent steps of responding to their communication must be good enough to convert them into a paying client.

Some enquirers have made up their mind and will simply want to book a session without needing to ask questions. Others will ask from one to a dozen questions before they will make a decision. Remember that as long as they ask questions, they are interested. Answer their questions and reassure them and you will get another appointment time filled.

Answering questions successfully

Most of the questions asked by enquirers you will have heard before, and you should have tried and tested answers. On a website there will often be a page dedicated to FAQs or 'Frequently Asked Questions' for this very reason. Some questions may surprise you. If this happens don't blurt out some waffle. Take your time in responding. Use the old tactic of repeating the question back to the caller, which will give you more time to think about the answer. Never lie or make promises that you cannot deliver. If you genuinely cannot answer a question say so. They will have more belief in you because of your honesty.

Organisations often use telesales teams who are given a script to read to customers. This provides a uniform standard of customer communication across the company. Although your response should not be rigid, memorising a standard response will be helpful. It gives you more confidence and it sounds to the client you know what you are talking about.

Communicating the session fees

If a client asks you how much a session costs, do not blurt out the price straightaway. Say to them, 'Can I tell you what is involved in a session so that you know what you are paying for?' This gives you control: you can outline the benefits of your service before mentioning your charges. Tell them what a session involves and include any extras such as a free consultation. At the end say something like 'and your investment in your health is £50'. But do not let the '£50' float around in their mind. After informing them of the cost, immediately ask them 'Do you have any other questions I can help you with?' If you do this they are not left with £50 stuck in their mind but are thinking if they need any other information.

Prepare set responses

If you get an enquiry by email, have some prepared responses ready. This saves a lot of time and also ensures you don't forget any important details. You can always personalise your response by including their name and answering specific questions not covered in your standard reply. The same procedure is applicable to writing letters to potential clients. Always enclose your practice brochure when corresponding by letter.

13

TALKING TO CLIENTS ON THE TELEPHONE

Your marketing effort continues with the telephone. If you can have a dedicated telephone line just for your therapy practice, so much the better. This way you will always know that when the telephone rings it will be a business call and you can answer it in a professional manner. Other members of the family will also know to leave the telephone for you to answer or to take a message in an appropriate way.

Handling calls when you are busy

Potential clients may telephone you when you are in a therapy session, are out elsewhere or when you are using the telephone. To cover for this eventuality some therapists use a telephone bureau. The bureau takes your calls for you in a professional manner. The potential client always gets to talk to a person as opposed to a machine. The bureau will also book clients for you if you provide them with the information about how to handle your calls. There is a charge for this service that on average is about £50 per month. If your fees are £50 and you receive one extra booking a month through using this service (that you might have otherwise lost) it will pay for itself.

If you decide that the telephone bureau is not appropriate, for whatever reason, invest in an answering machine or service. Many telephone companies provide an answering service and will record a message (even if you are using the telephone at the time) rather than just give the caller an engaged tone. If the caller cannot contact you, then the next best option is an answering machine or service. If they just get no answer, they may give up and seek out another therapist.

When you pick up your telephone messages, you must telephone the client back as soon as you can. Even though they have left you a message and contact number, that doesn't mean that they are going to wait for you to telephone back. Some clients ring around a number of therapists and will book an appointment with the first therapist they speak to.

Not all clients will want to leave a message, so another useful facility is a redirection service. All calls from your business telephone can be re-routed through to your mobile or other telephone by punching in a special code. If you are available to take those calls this is an excellent way of not missing any potential clients.

Easy to remember

Your telephone number can also help your marketing. You can purchase personal numbers that equate to words or form memorable numbers. It is much easier for a client to remember 07777 29 29 29 than 060 7967 29783. Memorable numbers are particularly useful with a radio marketing campaign.

14

OFFERING A FREE PHONE NUMBER

You can encourage potential clients to contact you by making a free telephone service available. This can sometimes make the difference between someone taking action or not. It gives the added incentive that by telephoning you for more information they are not losing anything because the telephone call is free.

Advantages

If you are able to boast a free phone number it does enhance your public persona. It gives the impression that this business takes itself seriously, is professional and will be around for some time. A free phone number also deals with a small objection that some people may have – i.e. the cost of the call.

You can enhance your 'pulling power' even further if you manage to obtain a free phone number that is memorable.

Increased costs

The negative side of a free phone number is that your business pays for the customer's call and there is an additional service charge on top of this. You might also wonder, if a person is unwilling to spend a few pennies on a telephone call, how will they cope when you tell them your therapy fees? Some existing customers may take advantage of the free phone by using it for purposes such as cancelling appointments, rearrangements and general queries.

In order to keep your costs under control you will need to make it clear that existing customers must use a different telephone number. You can achieve this by calling the free phone number an 'information' line and emphasising that its use is only for new clients who are considering therapy.

15

RETAINING CLIENTS

Having attracted a client to your practice through one of your many marketing ideas, now is not the time to lose the plot. Everything you do with this client from the first telephone call to the last goodbye, must ooze quality and professionalism.

Help clients relax quickly

You can help clients to relax by building rapport quickly, but don't get over friendly. There is a fine line between keeping the interaction jovial and warm and stepping over the line into treating the client like a buddy. They are the 'customer' and you are the 'provider' of a service. They want the best for their money. If you let your professional persona drop during the session, there is the possibility that you will lose your concentration and become sloppy.

Listen to your clients

If you have an unhappy client do not reach for the book of excuses, just listen to them. They want to know that you have understood why they are unhappy. If you feel the client has a genuine complaint, then take action to make amends. If they don't have a good reason for a complaint then you need to be firm in explaining your point of view.

For every single unhappy client who expresses their disappointment, research has shown that there are at least another six in existence who have been unhappy but have not said anything to you. These clients will never come back to you but they may tell others about their dissatisfaction. The one client who has complained has actually done you a favour. They have pointed out a problem and if you correct it, this can prevent you from losing many more clients. When you look at it this way, you can see that it is well worth your while making the effort and meeting the expense of regaining the good will of that unhappy client.

Often, if you make amends, the client who complained can become your best referral source. You have made them feel valued and have cared about their issues, and this can really transform how someone feels about you and your therapy.

16

SPECIALISING

If you had a particular ailment and you wanted to see a therapist for help, you would want to know that the therapist had expertise or at least some experience in that area. It really can pay huge dividends for you to have a more in-depth knowledge of a particular ailment and the techniques to help.

Often an area of specialisation selects you. For some reason therapists seem to attract certain clients and certain ailments. Sometimes you may find a niche thrust upon you. However, you can also decide that you would like to focus on people who have eczema, for example. The more you study and make this ailment your own special area, the more your therapy skills will be refined and the more people you can help.

After a time you will find that you become known as the person to see if you have eczema. This reputation not only builds amongst potential clients but also with your fellow therapists. You may even find your colleagues in the same field referring their clients with eczema to you.

Specialising does not stop you from helping the usual collection of problems but adds a new dimension to your marketing. Clients who know you have good results with one ailment will assume that you are just as successful in other areas. There is nothing quite like the reputation of an expert to help your practice keep busy through personal recommendations.

Becoming a perceived expert in a certain ailment can also help you to increase your income in other areas. You can give lectures to existing therapy schools as master classes for their therapists. You can also provide your own independently run workshops.

With more experience you will start to use the language that medical experts use to describe aspects of the ailment. In any communication with these experts or other bodies it can reassure them that you do know what you are talking about and will give you a better chance of getting the message across that you do have something worthwhile to contribute.

17

ASSISTING RECOMMENDATIONS

When you have your client's attention, and the opportunity arises, include in the conversation examples of how you have helped other people. The best time is when you are chatting at the outset to a new client. In order to help them know that you get results, you can give anecdotal examples of your success. Also do this when they have finished their session and you are back to 'small talk' before they leave your practice. Rather than talking about the weather or how bad the traffic is, why not talk about a success story.

When the client says at the end of their therapy, 'Thanks, I really enjoyed that,' you can say, 'Good, but you know, NLP never ceases to amaze me. Only recently I helped someone who lacked confidence for years to get their life back together. They are now running their own successful business.' A hypnotherapist might say, 'Quite recently I helped someone overcome their needle phobia which used to prevent them from going to the dentist.'

These anecdotes plant a seed in the client's mind. The client might not have come because of confidence or a phobia but they will eventually meet someone who has got one of these issues and they may say, 'I know someone who can help you with that.'

By taking the time to mention other ailments you have successfully treated, you gain the assistance of your current client with your marketing effort. Everyone loves to feel knowledgeable and to give advice. Your client gets to feel good by informing someone of a therapist who may be able to help them.

18

PROVIDING TESTIMONIALS

People feel more secure knowing that they are not the first person you have seen for a particular problem. They want to know that you have expertise and have had success in the areas with which they need help.

Nothing helps with this more than having some testimonials ready to show your clients. For those clients who are undecided at the initial consultation, the production of a few testimonials can work wonders.

If you are going to show any correspondence you have received from happy clients you must have their permission, otherwise your confidentiality guarantee will be compromised. If you still want to show testimonials but don't have permission from the client, then cover up the name and address details. The easiest way to do this is to photocopy the testimonials and black out the identifying details. The reader can then see that the testimonial is real but cannot see who sent it.

Quoting testimonials

On your leaflet include a few quotes from those letters and cards, but again keep them anonymous. If you want to refer to the person, do so by their ailment.

> 'I was so relaxed travelling to Sydney, Australia . . .'
> *flying phobia*

> 'I feel so much more in control of my life . . .'
> *executive stress*

> 'The pain has gone completely . . .'
> *joint pain*

You can also show these quotes from satisfied clients on your website, posters, brochures, leaflets, mini-manuals and advertisements (see Chapter 3 for more on these).

19

PLAYING IT COOL

If you are not getting enough clients and are desperate for the telephone to ring, make sure that this does not become apparent in your manner or voice. Nothing will drive a client away faster than the impression that you don't have many clients and will do anything to encourage someone to come along. 'Anything', does not mean marketing. Doing 'anything' can mean promising the client 'the earth' when you know that you cannot or are not sure that you can help them. Another mistake is to give the impression that you have plenty of appointments available. The client will conclude that if you are available to see them at any time, you don't have many clients and must therefore be a poor therapist.

Clients gain confidence in your skills if they get the impression that you are very busy. Busy equates to being successful and having a good reputation. Always talk as if you have a full practice, even if you only see three people a week.

Your fees should be set and you should not be too willing to compromise on price. There will always be exceptions but you should try to stick to your fee structure. If you reluctantly allow yourself to be negotiated to lower fees by a client they will have the impression that your services are not valuable and therefore not the best quality and you will feel resentful towards the client because you are not getting your full fee.

Be willing to let clients go, and recommend other forms of help if they show any doubt about visiting you. The more you show that you are willing to let them make up their own mind the more they will believe that you are the person they should see. Just as with parents of teenagers, if you try to hold on to them, they will push you away, but if you let them go, they will come back of their own accord.

The impression you aim to give to everyone is of a practice that is successful and busy. You welcome new clients but you are not desperate for their business.

MANAGING YOUR PRACTICE

Every 3 months take some time out to review your practice management.
Make changes and additions as your experience continues to grow to refine your customer interaction into a smooth and easy operation.

Creating Promotional Materials

It is essential to spend some time getting your promotional materials designed and produced to the highest quality your budget can afford. These materials are your 'shop window' to the world.

There are some information media that are essential to getting your name known and creating the right impression.

All organisations, whether a business, charity, government body or other, use paper-based materials to provide information. The materials in the form of posters, leaflets, booklets or flyers convey important information to the users and potential users of the services available.

Your business and your therapy practice need to provide the same.

20

DESIGNING A PRACTICE BROCHURE

A brochure is an important aspect of your marketing. In fact it is probably the number one item in your marketing armoury. It conveys so much about you. A business card displays a small amount of information whereas a therapist's brochure includes so much more and could persuade a client to see you.

Essential details for your brochure

■ Your name

■ Your contact details
  – Telephone number
  – Email address
  – Website address

■ Your practice address in full or just the area you are located in

■ Your qualifications

■ Details of training schools (if appropriate)

■ Membership of any relevant organisations

■ Type(s) of therapy you offer

■ Benefits of your therapy

■ Ailments and problems you can help with

■ Answers to frequently asked questions

■ Details of sessions

Putting your brochure together

If you are not sure about style and layout, go to your local library and obtain other therapists' brochures. They will give you some ideas. Most of such brochures are made up of three parts, although some therapists use two parts. A three-part brochure is simply an A4 sheet of paper, turned on its side (landscape) and folded into thirds.

The front of your leaflet needs to communicate an immediate point of interest to a potential client. Ask questions and highlight benefits. Do not splash your name in the biggest typeface. Potential clients are not interested in your name, or at least not initially. They will want to know that you can help them. Use something like Figure 3.

These examples are quite specific and offer help for stress or a lack of confidence. Do not overcrowd the front page; keep it snappy and to

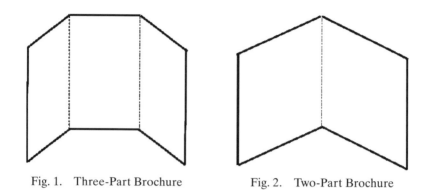

Fig. 1. Three-Part Brochure   Fig. 2. Two-Part Brochure

the point. Your contact telephone number should be on the front and repeated elsewhere in the brochure. Use at least 100gsm quality paper. You may want to keep your multi-coloured brochures for this purpose. However, if you are going to distribute hundreds of brochures, then the quality can drop to 80gsm and black print on coloured paper will suffice.

It can be useful to have your marketing leaflets checked by the National Advertising Standards Authority to make sure you are not breaking advertising guidelines.

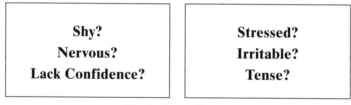

Fig. 3. Front Page

21

CREATING BUSINESS CARDS

Well-designed business cards indicate that you are serious about what you do and convey an air of respectability and professionalism. Do not go anywhere without them. You will be surprised how often you will find yourself in a situation where there is an opportunity to secure a client. Scraps of paper with your details scrawled on them will more than likely end up lost or discarded. A business card in a customer's wallet or purse will be a constant reminder of your service.

Essential details for your business card

- Your name
- Any designations
- Your profession
- Telephone numbers
- Email address
- Website address
- Postal address

Extra details (on the back)

- A mini appointment schedule
- Rules of the practice (24 hour notice of cancellation, etc.)
- List of ailments you treat

Quality counts

Your business card must be a high-quality product. The weight of the card should be no less than 120gsm. The layout of the information must be neat, consistent and pleasant to look at. Your name, profession and telephone number will need to be in a larger typeface compared to other information.

Marketing with your business cards

Consider all the opportunities you have to offer your business card to others:

- Dropping the children off at school

- Doing the weekly grocery shop

- At a football match

- Attending a reunion of old school chums

- At a family gathering

Keep a supply in your wallet, purse or handbag, in any jackets and in the glove compartment of the car. Give your spouse or partner a supply because they may be asked for one. In other words, never miss an opportunity to distribute your business cards.

22

LEAFLETING

This is an area that seems so obvious, yet many people don't even consider it. One of the reasons is that the majority of leaflets pushed through letter boxes get thrown away. You have only a few seconds to grab someone's attention, as per the AIDA principles referred to on pages 81–2.

Numbers count

To be successful with this marketing tool you need to deliver several thousand leaflets as a minimum. It can work for you, but you need to consider whether this is an appropriate medium for the image you are trying to project. It will not appeal to all types of therapy. A counsellor may decide that this type of promotion does not reflect well on their service but a chiropractor may find it appropriate and effective.

Designing your leaflet

An A5 size leaflet is big enough to be noticed and include all the relevant details and is less expensive than an A4 leaflet. Choose a colour of paper that you feel reflects the message you are trying to get across. Do not choose bright pinks or fluorescent colours. Black or dark blue ink makes the typeface easy to read. Emphasise the benefits and consider including a discount coupon with a 'Use by' date. Make it easy for clients to contact you.

Now add up the total costs of producing and distributing the leaflets. If you divide this total cost figure by your client fee, you get an idea of how many clients you need to attract in order to break even. Generally, you could expect a response of about a quarter to a half of one percent. For every thousand leaflets delivered, you could expect between two and five clients.

Of course, those two clients might attend for three sessions and recommend you to their friends. These are other variables to take into account when deciding if this marketing method is a winner for you or not.

23

SELLING THERAPY PRODUCTS

Most therapies will use items that can be supportive of the therapy. These items can be sold to the general public to increase your revenue but they can also be another way of marketing yourself.

Write a book

They say that everyone has a book in them and it is no different for the therapist. The subject of the book could be anonymous case histories, or a 'How to do it in three easy steps' manual, or your own methods of enhancing an existing therapy. Having a book published elevates your standing in the eyes of the public. There is a perception that you must be an expert in your field if you have written a book about the subject. This perception can help attract clients to your door as well as the book earning you income in its own right.

Other side products

You can also sell other products. A hypnotherapist could sell self-hypnosis tapes. An aromatherapist might sell essential oils and oil burners. If your therapy is more practical, you could market a video of aromatherapy techniques aimed at a section of the community such as couples. A massage therapist could produce a video about baby massage or make up individual combinations of massage oils for clients. All these items give you a chance of increasing your marketing effectiveness and also your income.

All your therapy products can be listed for sale on your practice brochure and on your website. You could even have a display of these products in your practice room or, if working at a clinic, in the reception area. This way you can earn an income even if you are not in the clinic. If the product is of a good quality and packaged well, you might even persuade local health shops to display and sell it for you.

Many therapists play soothing and relaxing background music while seeing a client. Clients subconsciously make an association between the music played and the good feelings they get when experiencing the therapy. With this in mind, clients may ask you where they can obtain the music. You could sell CDs, cassettes and mini-discs – another opportunity to add to your income.

24

PUBLISHING YOUR OWN NEWSLETTER

With the advent of easier and cheaper ways of producing documents to a professional standard, it is quite feasible to produce your very own newsletter. The idea of the newsletter is ultimately to promote your practice and to bring more clients to your door. However, it needs to offer a community information service.

Suitable newsletter contents

- Topical and supportive stories paraphrased from national newspapers or magazines (be aware of copyright infringements)

- Informative articles about your therapy
  – history
  – development

- Competitions

- Workshop details

- Advertising

- A list and descriptions of your therapy products

- Your contact details

- An appropriate name for the newsletter (e.g *Utopia, Tranquillity Times*, etc.)

The newsletter should include articles of an informative nature and should not be a purely promotional document. Libraries and health shops will not take any literature that is just sales material unless, in the case of a health shop, it is promoting an item they are selling.

Strike a balance between information and promotion. Have articles that talk about the causes of stress and give the top ten tips for reducing stress. One of the tips might be to take up a relaxation practice. If you are a yoga teacher, then mention yoga as a stress buster. If you are a life coach, describe how your skills can help to identify the causes of procrastination and to reduce or eliminate them.

Newsletters tend to take advertisements to help with the costs of production. You can legitimately place a reasonable number of ads in the newsletter; just ensure that they are not in direct competition with you.

Ideally, the newsletter should be at least a B3 size but folded in half to form a booklet of A4 size. This is large enough to allow space for interesting articles, to take advertising and to include details of your treatments, courses and any workshops. Choose quality coloured paper (at least 100gsm) and colours like cream, light blues or greens. Incorporate some pictures or diagrams to break up the text and add interest.

25

PRODUCING MINI-MANUALS

Producing a mini-manual about your therapy is a way of guiding the novice through the basics. The manual can be similar to the classic publications, 'How to play Golf in three easy stages', ' The Lazy Man's Guide to Gardening' or 'How to give a Best Man's Speech'.

A mini-manual can be sold at fairs, via mail shots for a small fee or it can be given away to increase your client numbers. It can act like the bait on a fishing line. A small fish is used to attract and reel in a bigger fish. A mini-manual should not go into fine detail. It should just describe the basic process and may incorporate diagrams to make it an easy read – something that someone could read in an hour perhaps and get a better idea of how they can use the therapy.

The manual should include details of what can be expected from undergoing the full therapy in the hands of a professional therapist. In other words, it should describe what you can do and the benefits clients will receive from a visit to you. You should also include contact details such as telephone number and email address. In order to get the reader to take action you may want to offer them a discount if they use a coupon in the manual.

You can encourage local traders to take advertising space in the manual. Approach appropriate traders such as health shops, chemists and other non-competitive therapists. Using this strategy you can recover some of your production costs.

Once the mini-manual has been put together with no more than 10 to 15 pages, all your hard work is done. Reproduction does not have to be of an excessively high quality, although you might want to spend more resources on the attractiveness of the front and back pages. With the availability of desktop publishing you may decide to produce copies as and when required. If you have a large event coming up consider getting a professional printer to reproduce your mini-manual.

Some ideas for mini-manuals

■ 12 Ways to Help You Stop Smoking

■ 12 Ways to Help You Reduce Your Stress

■ 6 Easy-to-Learn Massage Strokes

■ 24 Aromatherapy Oils That Can Change Your Life

CREATING PROMOTIONAL MATERIALS

Never underestimate the effectiveness of distributing leaflets, business cards and other paper-based marketing materials if they have been designed well. The use of these can be one of the easiest and most consistent ways of attracting new clients.

Educating The Masses

Learning establishments of all types play a useful role for the creative therapist and may even provide the backbone for a thriving private practice.

People love to learn and increase their knowledge. One of the most popular goals is to learn a new skill. Existing educational bodies such as schools and colleges can provide a ready-made class including fee collection, environment and promotion for the budding therapist who wants to teach.

Of course you do not have to be restricted to the structure imposed by your local college. Many therapists run their own courses and workshops ranging from one day to a number of years' duration and have their own fee structure. There are also numerous ways of teaching and training people.

26

PUTTING ON A FUNDRAISING EVENT

The PTAs (Parent–Teacher Associations) of schools are always putting on events to raise extra income. The budget that a school receives from government or the local authority is never sufficient and events to raise extra funds can make quite a real difference to school life. The hardest part for a PTA is constantly to think of new schemes, ideas and events to encourage the parents and other members of the public to support the school.

Put yourself in the PTA's shoes and create a way of using your therapy to help boost the school's funds. For a hypnotherapist it could be to offer to run a group 'Stop Smoking' session. You could charge a fee of £20 per person and state that all monies will go to the school. Get the local media involved: radio, television, newspapers and the school newsletter.

Costs to you

- A couple of hours of your time
- Production of extra brochures

Benefits to you

- You will get free publicity for your therapy practice (try paying for that exposure in the media and you will realise what a bargain you have got!).
- The local community will love you because of your fundraising skills (also helping your reputation and image).
- Attendees and others will want to take away your therapy brochure and may contact you later for help with other issues (always carry your brochures with you).
- People may want to continue the work they started in the £20 session by coming to see you privately.

If the session is successful, people will spread the word. People talk more easily to others about a public session than if they had visited you for a more private reason.

Ideas for different therapies

- Life coach – provide a motivation seminar.
- Massage therapist – teach couples simple strokes to help each other relax.
- Reflexologist – teach a basic routine.

■ Nutritionist or homeopathist – give a talk on natural remedies for ailments.

Always have plenty of brochures, take your diary with you and encourage the local media to cover the event.

27

27. WORKING WITH SCHOOL TEACHERS

There is a myth that teachers work from 9am to 3.30pm and have about 12 weeks' holiday a year. The truth is that teachers can start their day any time before 9am and finish around 5pm or much later. Then when they get home they spend their evening marking school work. They spend parts of their weekend planning lessons for the following week or catching up on administrative tasks that seem to be constantly increasing. Add to this the hassle they can get from unruly pupils, demanding parents, head teachers and governors and you may begin to understand why so many teachers reach burnout, suffer a breakdown and leave the profession.

Stress is the number one issue for teachers today. Although teachers do have set-aside training days, these are mostly related to the school curriculum. Few training days – if any – help teachers to cope with the demands of being a teacher. You can imagine that anyone or any organisation that can help teachers to reduce their stress levels and to relax more is going to be of interest to them.

Approaching head teachers

This could be the opportunity for you to offer your services. You could put together a one-day training course and help teachers as a group.

1. Write to the head teachers of your local schools.
2. Detail the range of benefits your therapy offers and state what the school, teachers and pupils will gain through your therapy.

3. A week after your letter has been sent, follow it up with a telephone call.

4. Give examples of your past successes, if you can.

Another idea is to arrange to visit the school on a regular basis and provide individual sessions. A practitioner who provides Indian head massage could visit the school during the lunch break and offer this service to some teachers in the staff room. Another possibility is for teachers to enjoy your therapy when they are given non-contact time (time out of the classroom).

There are many ways in which you could reach an agreement with a school to help with stress levels. You will, of course, find that head teachers, caretakers, school governors and parents will also become curious and want to use you as well. Just imagine the possibilities of word spreading beyond the school about how good your service is. This is a great way to build your personal referral network.

Getting more from your course

Once you have put together a half- or one-day course and have presented it, you will have a tried and tested service which you can offer to many other establishments. All you need to do is change the emphasis of the target audience, in this case from teachers, to, for example, nurses, the police, fire crew, office workers, traffic wardens, social workers and more.

28

WORKING WITH SCHOOL PUPILS

Children of all ages can suffer from stress and tension and there is no doubt that this impacts on their performance in the classroom. It can also affect their relationships with fellow pupils, teachers and parents.

If there was a way to help the whole school enjoy some mental and physical relaxation, then there could only be positive results. The pupils would operate from a calmer disposition and the number of disagreements and squabbles would be reduced. The mind absorbs more information when it is relaxed. Learning new material would become easier and quicker. Retrieving that information for examinations would also be easier because recall is more efficient when the mind and body are relaxed.

For the NLP practitioner this kind of opportunity should be very easy. Visualisation coupled with the other senses is a great way of altering a person's state of mind, helping them to drift off into a reverie or daydream. The visualisation can contain some meaning or lesson (such as truth, honesty, respect for each other, etc.) which can be absorbed by the subconscious mind, adding even more to the event.

Usually, if a story of any kind is read to a class, it tends to be the last lesson of the day. If it were possible for these visualisation sessions to be held first thing in the morning, it could get the whole day off to a better start.

Not all therapies will be appropriate in this area but many can be, with a little creativity. For instance, an aromatherapist could help the children with progressive relaxation exercises. This can simply be tensing and relaxing muscle groups one by one, from the toes to the head and back again. They could advise on the best aromatherapy oils for concentration and memory enhancement.

If the pupils, no matter what age, were to start their day from a calmer place, their resources, such as memory, attitude, focus, and motivation could be greatly improved. This in turn would help the teachers with their stress levels and could really enhance school life for everyone.

29

WORKING IN COLLEGES AND UNIVERSITIES

You can take all the ideas we have looked at for schools and duplicate them for colleges, universities and any other educational establishments.

However, at these places of learning you have people who are young adults and are responsible for themselves.

Recognising the needs of your target group

Some of these young adults or students will want help to cope with college life. This help might be in the usual areas of relationships, fears and lack of confidence, but many will want help with studying. If you can devise a programme to help students with studying, retaining and retrieving information and their examinations, then you will be a very popular resource.

You may opt to offer group sessions where attendees are charged a flat fee, or individual sessions with interested students. First, though, you need to let the students know that you exist and what it is that you can do for them.

Approaching a college or university

Initially, try the official route through the college hierarchy. It is easier to convince them of your skills if you can boast about a previous course at another college. But, of course, you have to start somewhere. Be sure you have given prior thought to the course structure and are able to present the outline. All colleges want their students to get the highest grades, so in your initial approach emphasise how you can help with this.

Despite your good intentions and the obvious benefits, you might still get turned away. Your next strategy is to approach the Student Union. Tell them that you will provide a discounted course if they organise the venue and publicise the event. The Student Union's job is to look after their members' welfare. Hint at this aspect when you contact them. If you do get an agreement to provide a course, this will help you the following year if you decide to approach the college authorities again.

If none of the above succeeds, you can still display your notices around the college for individual sessions. Most students are short of cash so offer a reduction in fees for group sessions. For the next academic year you have gained evidence that your therapy has been used – ammunition when you approach the Student Union or college again.

Lastly, consider asking the college to provide a small room on the campus where you can offer discounted sessions to students. If you arrange to be available in this room, on a certain day and between set times this makes it as easy as possible for the students to find you and gives you the chance to build your reputation.

30

LIAISING WITH TRAINING SCHOOLS

Anyone who takes their practice seriously will have taken a course at a recognised school and passed some form of examination. Once you have qualified there is a temptation to go out there and have little or no contact with the school. If you do this, you could be missing out on opportunities to increase your income.

Gaining referrals

Any school of good standing will have potential clients contacting them and asking for a referral to a therapist. If you maintain good relationships with your school you will obtain some of these referrals. The better the school knows you, the more confidence they will have in passing these enquiries to you.

When you are approached by someone who has been referred to you by your training school, always let the school know that you have successfully made contact with this person and that you have taken them on as a client. This assures the school that you are dealing with their enquiries in a professional manner and gives them the confidence to pass more clients your way.

Returning the favour

You can help the flow of referred clients by building a reciprocal arrangement. If you are asked to recommend a school, assuming you have been happy with your training, make sure that you not only recommend your school but that you ensure the school knows that you have done this. Get the potential student to tell the school that they heard about it through you.

When invitations arrive to mix or socialise with new students and lecturers, grab the opportunity. This is another way of keeping your name and face known at the school and keeping those referrals flowing.

31

LECTURING

If you have ambitions towards lecturing at your training school or any other school, there are ways to help you achieve this that can also bring client referrals.

Giving your time to gain referrals

Volunteer to be an assistant on a relevant training course. You will usually only be allowed to perform this function if you have already taken and passed the course. Lecturers and tutors are always grateful for a spare pair of hands, particularly when it comes to the practical side of the course. Don't expect to get paid because you have volunteered but sometimes you may get a pleasant surprise! Remember you are getting invaluable experience at running a course for free!

Assisting on a course gives you an easy way of learning about different styles of lecturing, how a course is structured and how to manage the students. It is just one step away from running the course yourself. In an emergency the school will probably ask you to attend if the lecturer is ill or can't make it for any reason.

You can always ask the lecturer if there are any parts you can be more active in, once you have attended the course as an assistant and are feeling confident about the subject area. For example, if the module of the course is on physiology and anatomy you might want to volunteer to lecture on a part of that. This can be of great benefit to all concerned. The official lecturer gets a break but has the opportunity to intervene if they feel you have missed any important details. You get a brilliant opportunity to show your mettle as a lecturer. The students get to have someone different lecturing to them, which can help their attention and focus.

Finally, you will be perceived as an experienced therapist because you are assisting and lecturing. Students will seek your advice with their client cases. They may also pass some of the more difficult cases to you. Once more, you gain client referrals as a side effect of doing something else.

32

SUPERVISING STUDENTS

After gaining experience in your field, you could approach your old therapy school, or any other school for that matter, and find out whether they need any new supervisors. In order to give yourself a chance of success with your approach, you must be able to prove that you have experience of being supervised. The frequency and type of supervision will vary between different schools and therapies.

Schools of good repute will have guidelines about the qualities and experience needed to become a supervisor. They should also provide a course to train you to supervise individuals and groups. Many therapy schools are now insisting that students receive supervision while they are attending a therapy course and some insist on supervision after the course is completed. For counsellors, psychotherapists and now hypnotherapists, supervision is seen as a necessity.

Adding a new dimension to your practice

Supervised sessions are paid for by the person involved. The cost to the person being supervised (student or graduate) is generally lower than for a client's therapy session, but for a supervisor it can be a useful additional income. Indeed, it can also lead to more clients. Students will come in contact with clients who have issues they feel are beyond them at their current stage of experience. The students are highly likely to pass these clients on to their supervisors. As a supervisor you can earn supervisory fees as well as gaining clients referred to you by those students.

Build up a good relationship with your students and when they graduate you may find that they still want to come to you for supervision and recommend others to do the same.

33

RUNNING EVENING CLASSES

Running a class gives you the chance to enjoy passing on your skills to others and have some security regarding your income. An evening class is usually for a set number of weeks. The financial security is gained by charging attendees in advance for the duration of the course. The class can run for six weeks, a college term, or the whole academic year. This is your choice and there are a number of ways of organising this.

Local adult education authorities are always looking for new courses to offer the community. You increase chances of your course being accepted if you are clear about areas you want to teach, can support this by emphasising the benefits attendees will gain, and have a structure of how you want to teach it.

To give you confidence, you really need to have a clear idea of what you are going to do during each class. After each session the students should leave having learnt something new and of value. If you attempt to 'pad out' your course to fill the time, this will become obvious and students will give you a poor rating when they are asked to assess the course.

If you do put together a good course and are turned down by the local authority, all is not lost. There is nothing to stop you hiring a venue and providing a private group course if you feel there is a market for it.

The advantages of the local authority are that they are responsible for all the marketing, administration and providing a room. The disadvantage is that they will stipulate the fee that you can charge per student and you will not necessarily receive all of this.

The advantages of running a private class are that you can decide what to charge and are not restricted by term times. The disadvantages are that you have to market the course and hire a venue.

Although running a course can be financially rewarding in itself, there are other ways that you can gain. Some students will want to see you for one-to-one treatment, while others will pass on your details to potential clients. The possibility of gaining more private work is therefore increased.

34

ORGANISING MONTHLY GROUPS

Once a month, organise a group of five or six people (however many you can fit into your practice room) to learn the basics of your therapy. Charge them some nominal fee for attendance and make it more of an informal occasion than a serious private session.

Training for basic skills

The idea of the group is not to train people to set up professionally but to acquaint them with the basics so that they could make use of their knowledge on a spouse, partner, friend or themselves. This will not take business away from you because you are merely showing them what they can achieve with a little knowledge. If the person they practise on enjoys the basics of the therapy they may well come to see you to get the full professional treatment.

Make sure your practice brochures are available, as members of the group may want to see you privately. Ensure they all go away with your business card because they will talk about what they learnt to work colleagues, family and friends and provide another opportunity to gain referrals.

The group meeting should be no longer than three hours and an evening is generally the most popular time. Having the meeting once a month gives you plenty of time to prepare and also doesn't interfere with your private practice.

Ideas for groups

- Aromatherapist – give talks about different oils and their therapeutic qualities.

- NLP therapist – help the group recognise old outdated patterns. Show ways of replacing them with effective life strategies.

- Shiatsu practitioner – talk about the theory. Show some simple techniques.

As the therapist you get paid for your time and expertise and you increase the possibility of more client referrals. If the evenings become very popular you may need to look for a bigger venue but the increase in attendance fees should cover any expense.

35

OFFERING CORPORATE WORKSHOPS

There are in existence thousands of companies of different sizes and shapes. With the exception of sole traders they all have one thing in common: they employ people. They need people in order to be successful and so you might say that people are their number one asset.

People are complex beings and have different needs and wants. The importance of people to companies has become more evident and is reflected in the Personnel Department now being called the Human Resources Department. More companies are recognising that a happy and contented workforce can mean more efficient and effective employees which will then feed through positively into the bottom line – profits.

Helping to maintain a happy workforce

Companies are more open to ways of helping to keep their workforce happy and at their peak performance for as long as possible. They have recognised that it takes more than paying a weekly or monthly wage to do this. If you can recognise the needs of the company and its personnel, and offer a way of helping to fulfil those needs, then you increase your chances of securing corporate work.

Before your first approach, you must step into your customer's shoes and see matters from their perspective. What can you do for them? They want to know what benefit they will get from using your services. Once you have recognised the benefits you can provide you are ready to contact them.

Approaching companies

Companies vary tremendously in the number of employees they have and the profitability of the business, as well as their culture. What will appeal to one company will be rejected outright by another. Your initial approach must be to find out the name of the person who has the power to say yes or no to your service. Telephone the company and ask the operator for the name of someone in the Human Resources Department. Have a chat with the person concerned. The idea of this call is not, I repeat *not*, to find out if they are interested in your therapy. It is to find out who makes the decisions about workshops and courses for the company. You want the person's name and title. When you have this information you end the conversation by saying you will write to them.

Be clear on what you are offering the company. Don't be vague or give too much choice. Write a letter to the name you have acquired and follow the AIDA principles mentioned on pages 81–2. Enclose a brochure giving more details about the course you are offering and stating the price. This will save you having to put too much detail in the covering letter. Try to let them know that you are knowledgeable about their industry. The more they feel you understand them, the more likely they are to look at your service favourably.

When you send the letter, make a note in your diary to follow this up with a telephone call no longer than a week later. Following the letter with a telephone call shows that you mean business. If your contact says that they haven't had time to read your letter, tell them you will ring back the next day. If they have passed it on to someone else to deal with, find out that person's name and speak to them immediately. If you get a rejection, find out why. This will help you improve your approach to the next company.

Do not undersell yourself. Generally you can charge double and sometimes triple your normal private rate. Appearing cheap will not help their perception of the quality of your service. Training companies often charge per person or will state a price for up to five people and then 10 people, and so on.

Corporate work can be very rewarding financially. It may even take you away from individual private practice to providing purely group work.

36

WORKING WITH LOCAL COUNCILS

Just as there is scope to secure business from private clients and corporate clients so you should not overlook your local councils. Although every household and business comes under the jurisdiction of a particular council, you do not have to restrict yourself because of this. Contact the councils in the surrounding area that are within a reasonable travelling distance for you.

Councils have many departments to handle cleansing, rates, legal matters, recreation, traffic, political matters and education, to name a few. All these departments employ many people who could benefit from your therapy. Just as with corporations, you need to let councils know that you exist and what you can offer their employees. You can approach the Human Resources division and follow a similar marketing plan to that described under 'Offering Corporate Workshops' earlier in this chapter.

Keeping your finger on the pulse

Receiving a regular copy of the council's newsletter can be a very useful source of information. From this publication and any others, you will find out useful contact names within the council and also find out on what particular social matter the council is focussing. If you feel you are able to offer them a workshop to help with their latest initiative, then approach them. They will be more open to a service that supports their own schemes than if you were trying to start up some completely new initiative of your own.

If you manage to support a council initiative and secure a role for your therapy, many wonderful benefits can come your way. You may find that as the council promotes its own chosen causes, whether for internal (council employees) or external (the public) consumption, your name and therapy are included in the promotion. This gives you a higher profile in your local community. As a result you can find that you get a sudden influx of new private clients. Local newspapers are always looking for information on unusual activities in the area and you may just find yourself the subject of an article under a headline such as:

Council Uses Reiki to Heal Tensions

EDUCATING THE MASSES

Focus on getting one training course or workshop and a promotion publication produced to support this idea. This will be your blueprint which over a period of time you can add to and subtract from and use to approach many education bodies.

Joining Directories

You must have your contact details in places where potential customers would expect to find you.

Directories of all sorts can provide free as well as 'value for money' opportunities for marketing. The majority of directories will offer a variety of options for listing your business – from a single text entry to a full-page display spread. With improvements in printing capabilities the choice extends beyond black and white to other text colours and even photographic images.

37

OPTING FOR *YELLOW PAGES*

For some time this publication has been the main source of finding anyone in any trade. How long this directory will remain a popular choice is anyone's guess, but with the advent of the internet and on-line directories it seems logical to conclude that its days may be numbered. However, that may still be somewhat in the future. The point is to remind you to think about how much return you are getting from your advertising budget and not to renew past contracts merely out of habit.

Taking an entry in *Yellow Pages* can be, with a few exceptions, a winner. Many people assume that any company or organisation that appears in *Yellow Pages* must be an established business and reasonably long term. The 'cowboys' tend to put a splash of adverts in a local newspaper today and are gone tomorrow. There is a kind of respectability that your business can enjoy from appearing in *Yellow Pages*.

Designing your advertisement

When it comes to designing your advert, as with all media, serious thought and consideration are needed. Although size isn't everything, it seems to make a difference here. The more impact you can achieve, the more clients will notice you and telephone your practice. Impact can be bought by having a bigger advert than your rivals. However, many advertisers spoil their entry by cramming too much detail into it. A customer scanning *Yellow Pages* will rarely bother with a crammed advert because it is not easy on the eye. Plenty of white space, or in this case yellow space, makes the text stand out and attracts the reader.

Look through different editions of *Yellow Pages* and particularly at the entries of your competitors. With your type of therapy or service there may be an accepted style. Go through the process of pretending to be a potential client. Based on the existing adverts decide which therapist you would go to and why their advert attracts you. This will give you the basis for your own design.

A medium-sized advert, with plenty of space, that has an emotional appeal and clearly states the essential details, will beat a larger and 'messy' advert every time. As humans we tend to make decisions based on emotions and afterwards arrive at a logical reason to support that decision. Aim for the emotions, but also include logic in the smaller details.

38

CHOOSING OTHER DIRECTORIES

There are many other directories published by different bodies and companies. While it is always a good idea to aim to let people know in as many places as possible that you exist, there are some common factors that can persuade you to decide for or against inclusion.

Estimating success from other directories

The number one factor is return on investment. You need to estimate the likelihood of anyone finding you in these directories. Compare like with like and contrast the cost and popularity. For example, there are other telephone directories that duplicate the service provided by *Yellow Pages*. The *Thomson Local* directory is in this category and has the added advantage that the directory is delivered to every household. *Yellow Pages* is delivered to households with telephones only. The rates for advertising in *Thomson Local* are lower than in *Yellow Pages* but, according to popular opinion, the majority of potential customers who have telephones turn to *Yellow Pages* first.

Other directories can be national or local. They may accept listings from certain businesses only. There are a number of complementary or alternative therapy directories in existence. The longer you are in business the more sales calls you will receive from these organisations trying to convince you that it is essential for the success of your business to be listed in their directory. Be careful here. It is so easy to get caught up in the hype and throw your advertising budget away.

Before committing yourself

1. Look at a copy of the directory.
2. Find out how, where and when the directory is distributed.
3. If certain establishments (libraries, clinics, etc.) are sent copies, check this out.
4. Telephone past advertisers and find out how successful their advert(s) has/have been.

Some directories are produced by therapy associations. An entry in such a directory is sometimes included in the annual membership fee or there may be a separate charge. It is well worth having an entry in your own association's directory, even if it is just a few lines.

39

ASSESSING TALKING PAGES

This service is currently run by *Yellow Pages* but there are other organisations such as Scoot that offer a similar service. Basically, a potential customer telephones Talking Pages and tells the operator the type of service they want to contact (Psychic, Colour Practitioner, etc.) and the location they want. The operator will then give the caller one business's telephone number and up to three others. The choice given to the customer depends on the number of businesses that are listed.

If you are the only business listed under your category, you will get all the customers that use this facility. If there are two businesses then your business will rotate between first and second place. It also means you are likely to receive half the business available through this medium. Even so, that might be more than adequate to be profitable.

Before committing yourself

1. Ask the company to provide statistics of the number of callers wanting your type of service in your location.
2. Pretend to be a customer and try the service.
3. Telephone the competition and see what they think of the service.

You cannot assume that just because a telephone number is accepted by the customer, they will actually call you. With this in mind, an additional service (with an additional cost) is now being offered where the caller is put directly through to your telephone. The idea is to sign up the customer while they are keen and to cut down on the possibility of their having second thoughts.

JOINING DIRECTORIES

Be on the look out for new directory opportunities. There is always someone creating a new and better medium for listing businesses.

Advertising Plus!

With adequate research and analysis, advertising can be profitable in the short and long term.

Many people make the mistake of thinking that marketing is simply advertising. Advertising of any sort is only a part of marketing, but an important one.

Advertising itself involves much more than just placing some information with contact details in a newspaper or magazine. As with everything there is an art to it. Follow the tips in this chapter to get the maximum return from your investment in advertisements.

40

ADVERTISING IN NEWSPAPERS

The thought may come to you as you read your daily newspaper and notice adverts for loans, courses and other products and services, that you could also promote yourself here. This isn't necessarily as silly as it may sound. It does depend on what you want to promote.

If your business consists of a practice in one location only, forget about advertising nationally. Your clients will not travel much beyond 10 or 15 miles to see you unless you have a national reputation or offer something that is a rarity or speciality. Realistically you should only expect to attract people from your locality, in which case you may as well stick to your local newspaper and get better coverage for your money.

Alternatively, if you have a number of practices around the country, if you are undertaking a national lecture tour or if you are selling a product via mail order, then national newspaper advertising could well be worth a longer look.

Tips for researching national advertising

1. Read and make notes (which detail the following points) from all the daily newspapers over the period of a week at least.
2. Who are the type of people who read each newspaper? Publications are available from any library's reference section that give these details. Generally, you will want to aim at people who have a reasonable disposable income.
3. When are the best days and which are the best sections in which to promote your therapy?
4. Is the newspaper running features or articles that could support your marketing?
5. Get your advert positioned close to any relevant articles.
6. Do not accept the first piece of space offered you.
7. Will a one-off or a series of adverts be more beneficial?
   – Look at other advertisers and see what they do.
   – Compare like with like.
   – Ask the newspaper advertising staff for their opinion.

Before designing your advertisement think about your target audience. Who is your client? If you aim at everyone your advert will not have any focus. Aim at the type of person or problem you want to help. Once you have decided who you are aiming at, there are a number of principles involved with advert design that are applicable to other promotional aids, such as posters, flyers and leaflets.

AIDA principles

'AIDA' stands for Attraction (or Attention), Interest, Desire, Action. Bear these principles in mind and your advert will be as effective as possible.

Attraction or Attention

You will have a very short space of time to attract your audience. If you don't get their attention, no matter how good the rest of your advert is, you will have lost your reader. Some of the better words to gain someone's attention are FREE or NEW or UNIQUE. Be brief with your attention grabber. Try to use less than five words. Never use the words 'I' or 'We' but use the word 'You' instead. Often an advert will ask a question and the idea is to get 'Yes' answers. For example, 'Are you stressed out?' If the reader responds with a mental 'Yes', they will feel that this advert is aimed at them and will read on.

Interest

Okay, you now have their attention and need to hold on to it. Readers get bored very quickly, so don't blind them with science. Think the way your reader thinks and put yourself in their position. Do not flog your cranio-sacral therapy at this point. Sell the 'sizzle' not the 'sausage'. Tell them that you can relieve headaches and migraines and release tension in their muscles.

Desire

In the 'interest' aspect you may have used negatives. In the 'desire' aspect, switch to positives such as 'feel calmer and more in control' or 'relax and take things in your stride'. In other words, you tap into the 'desire' of the reader to improve their life.

Action

This is where you encourage your reader to take action. Make it as easy as possible for them. At times people need to be told what to do next. Use action statements: 'To relax today telephone 0800 EASY LIFE now'. Highlight a 'Use by' date if you are making a special offer. This way people are more likely to take action now rather than miss out on the special deal. You could use the phrase, '20% discount to the first 20 callers on 0800 EASY LIFE'.

Thoughts for successful advert design

1. **Focus on your clients.**
   – Why would they come to you?
   – What will they gain?

2. **Highlight benefits more than features.**
   – You might be skilled in the latest techniques and have the most modern equipment but what will your client get from it?

3. **Work at your headline.**
   – Write a minimum of 20 headlines before deciding which one is best.
   – Include the most attractive words such as: Free, New, Amazing, Now, Announcing, How To, At Last, Here, Today.

4. **Use a relaxed style.**
   – Write using informal and/or local phrases.
   – Use short, punchy sentences.

5. **Drop the technicalities.**
   – Don't confuse the reader with jargon or mnemonics (unless you are using them to raise their curiosity).

6. **Don't write *War and Peace.***
   – Don't waffle or use 20 words when six will do.
   – Keep details focused.

7. **Give instructions.**
   – Tell them what to do: 'Phone Now' or 'Send the Completed Form Today'.

8. **Check it.**
   – Get someone to edit your advert for grammar and spelling.
   – Make sure obvious essential details are included (telephone number, address, etc.).

Other design tips

■ Make your advert easy to read by making sensible use of bold, italic and different sizes of typeface, but don't overdo it.

■ Use a mix of upper and lower case letters for headlines to make them easier to read.

■ The minor details at the bottom of the advert should include your name.

■ Include some designations but no more than four.

■ Incorporate words like 'professional', 'qualified', 'experienced' when referring to yourself.

Local newspapers

Here rates should be much lower and enable you to afford an advert that provides better exposure. But size isn't everything. You don't have to always use a display type advertisement. Sometimes the regular classified type of advertisement can be effective if you opt for a series over a number of weeks. Take a look at your rivals' adverts and decide which of them works best and why. Given the choice, which one would you want to telephone for an appointment? When you know why, then you are ready to design your own classified advertisement, but don't imitate – think how you can improve on your competition.

When you are ready to approach the newspaper to take advertising space, always ask for discounts. If you don't ask you won't get! In particular, when you want to place a display type advertisement enquire about the newspaper's policy on last minute space. This is when the deadline for printing is almost due but there is still space to be filled. Often the newspaper will give away the space at a much reduced rate in order to fill it. Sometimes you can be offered a whole page for the price that you would normally pay for a tenth of that size.

Whatever publication you decide to advertise in, always drive a hard bargain and make the most of your marketing budget.

41

INVESTIGATING MAGAZINES

Thousands of magazines are produced in the UK that focus on hundreds of subjects. There are also magazines imported from other countries. But just as with advertising in a national newspaper, if you are not careful you could easily be throwing your money away and learning a very expensive lesson.

Should I advertise in a national magazine?

Only if you can offer a product or service nationally should you consider advertising in a national magazine. The only exceptions to this rule are if your returns from local customers who find you through this medium are sufficient to cover your outlay, or your service is so specialised that people will be willing to travel the length or breadth of the country to consult you. You might be pleasantly surprised how far someone is willing to travel to see you as you become better known.

Choosing which magazines to advertise with is the next dilemma. For an aromatherapist who specialises in helping people with arthritis, it may be more obvious. An advert in *Arthritis Today* or any of the other publications on this subject may prove to be rewarding. On the other hand, a stress counsellor may want to advertise in *The Teacher*, which is a quarterly magazine. An osteopath may find advertising in a football magazine profitable.

To be successful, you must think about the type of person that reads the magazine and their lifestyle. From a profile of the reader, you should be able to conclude what service appeals to them. A beauty therapist may not have much return through advertising in a football magazine (although more women are attending football matches so it may well be a new and untapped opportunity). Time changes everything. Never restrict yourself with outdated stereotypes of the population. On the other hand, revolution can take time, so focus on certainties and take chances *only* once you are established and can afford to do so.

42

FOCUSING ON NEWSLETTERS

Here is a relatively inexpensive but focused way of getting your practice known. Newsletters exist in the thousands. With the advent of the computer and desktop printer, the production costs of newsletters have become so affordable that even the smallest group, organisation or society can put together a very respectable-looking publication. Newsletters vary in size, content and subject. Often the membership fees pay for the production of the newsletter and any income through advertising is a bonus to the organisation.

Although there are countless newsletters produced, obtaining a copy can be more difficult. If the organisation is private and has a closed membership you may never acquire a copy, unless you are a member or know someone who is a member. Alternatively, some organisations will supply copies of their current edition to local libraries. You should then be able to gain an idea of the content and decide whether placing an advert will be worthwhile.

Many people will keep every copy of a newsletter that they receive, particularly when the articles are interesting. So, although when you first advertise you may not get the response you hoped for, you could be pleasantly surprised at how many enquires you receive long afterwards.

Rates can vary tremendously, but because costs are lower and circulation is not large a display type advert should be quite affordable. You will probably be able to secure a decent-sized space and possibly be able to place it on the front or back of the newsletter for added exposure.

You can assist your marketing effort and gain more exposure if you can write an article that discusses your therapy and its relevance to the aims of the newsletter's organisation. You can negotiate with the editor for the amount of space you would like and may even want to make it a condition of advertising. The experienced negotiator may persuade the editor to give space for an article without having to purchase advertising space. Just as with newspapers, editors of newsletters find it difficult to find enough articles to fill the pages. You can use this to your advantage and save your marketing budget for something else.

43

RADIO BROADCASTING

Here is a medium that is often overlooked. Marketing via your local radio station can be more affordable than you think. The obvious approach is to consider advertising with the station. Some stations supply the whole package for you including a jingle and assistance with the best way to communicate your message. You also have the option of designing the commercial yourself.

Researching local stations

1. What choice of local radio stations do I have?
2. Which station attracts the biggest audience?
3. What type of audience does the station attract? (e.g. pensioners, mothers, teenagers, etc.) and at what times of the day?
4. What type of audience do I want my advertisement aimed at?
5. Do I want to use my voice or someone else's?
6. Should I include music and/or other sounds?
7. What is the message I am trying to get across?
8. What is the essential information I must mention? (contact details, location)

Spend some time listening to the local radio stations and the adverts in particular. This will give you ideas about the type of advertising that would best suit your service and how to present it in a professional way. The radio station should also be able to provide guidance to help you make the most of your air-time.

Gaining free exposure

Again, there is a way of gaining exposure without parting with any of your hard-earned money. Radio stations are always on the look-out for an interesting story or event. Simply use the same tactics that you used with your local newspaper and also refer to the sections on Articles and/or Competitions in this chapter. If you get involved with any charity event or with a school fundraiser, let the radio station know what you are doing. Inform them as soon as you can before it happens so that you and your practice gain the maximum exposure.

Another way of using the radio is to offer the station an informational programme. You could volunteer to be interviewed about your therapy, your practice and the issues you help with. If you are lucky, you might persuade some past clients to talk about how your therapy has helped them. Nothing promotes the benefits of your therapy more than firsthand accounts of real people's experiences. You might even encourage the station to produce a series of programmes about different complementary therapies. The result: you get free advertising and the radio station gets an interesting programme for its listeners. If you are good, you may even be able to turn it into a regular feature.

44

APPEARING ON TELEVISION

There are so many television channels broadcasting now that the opportunities to be on local or national TV are much easier. At times you may even be approached by a television company to appear on a particular programme.

Paid-for advertising is still very expensive and so the best way to market yourself on television is to be a guest on an appropriate programme. Think of all the chat shows there are now, morning, afternoon, evening and late-night shows. These shows might feature a certain type of therapy or be about a particular ailment. Often the subject of future programmes will be announced several weeks in advance. If you feel the subject is relevant to your therapy, contact the programme makers. If you can convince the makers that you can help with the subject area, you will not find it difficult to secure an invitation to join the programme.

Recently there has been a tendency to put together documentary programmes on the effectiveness of certain therapies in dealing with a particular problem. For example, the efficacy of hypnotherapy, NLP, cognitive therapy, counselling and others can be tested on people who have phobias. This is fine, as long as you get a result. Be aware that programme makers are only interested in a quick result and will have an effect on the therapy, just by being present. You really need to give careful consideration before allowing cameras into your therapy room. For those who do take this step the rewards can be an instant reputation and clients wanting to see you from all over the country. Generally, the client will be provided by the TV company and will be well aware of what is involved with regard to the lack of confidentiality. As the therapist you may also want to add your reassurance about how you will handle exceptional circumstances if they arise.

One therapist known to me appeared on a television programme about phobias and received over 200 calls from people who wanted her help with their phobia.

45

BILLBOARD ADVERTISING

Forget about the gigantic billboards that you see on the sides of buildings or alongside motorways as these would be highly unlikely to generate anything like the amount of business you would need to make them economically viable. The billboards that can be successful are those at your local bus station or railway station. If you live in a city you might consider the underground (in London) or other public transport systems for advertising.

Paying for billboards at stations that are not close to your practice location would be wasteful. Negotiate with the company responsible to rent the billboard at your local station. The best locations are the platforms at the station. Commuters and other travellers need something to do while waiting for the next train to arrive. This is your opportunity to capture their attention with a well-designed and well-placed advertisement.

The advertisement should let them know the benefits of treatment, the type of treatment you offer, ailments you help, a contact number and that you are a local business. In fact, you should cover a similar amount of detail to any of your other display advertisements. Do not overcrowd the space you have with too many details. Study other companies' designs and decide what you feel works, and what doesn't, to give you a better idea. Another option is to employ an expert to do this for you.

Other billboard locations

- Sheltered bus stops

- Local shopping centres

- Local airports

- Taxis and some mini-cabs

- Buses – on the inside and outside

46

USING LOCAL AUTHORITY PUBLICATIONS

Your local borough council or authority will have their own publications for communicating their goals and objectives to the local community. They will want to be seen to be supporting a local business because of the wider benefits this positive approach can bring in terms of direct revenue, jobs and custom for other businesses.

The editors of these publications will be interested in any article of an unusual nature. They can be quite supportive of your need for publicity, and give you space to promote yourself. The good news is that this is free publicity! It also gets you known to other businesses and may lead to some corporate work, where your fees can be on the higher side.

An added bonus is if your local council produces a glossy magazine of activities, events and news in the area. Copies of these magazines are provided to numerous local organisations and to public access facilities such as libraries and community projects. From this not only will local businesses become aware of your services but also the general public.

With this type of free publicity you can enjoy a perception of quality about your services. People will generally have the impression that your appearance in the council magazine means you must be professional, trustworthy and meet the highest standards.

Your approach to the editor of the magazine should be to request free editorial coverage – use the angle that you are letting them know about a new local service to the community. If your service is unique then you will have little problem in gaining that space. If you are offering something that is in abundance in your locality you will need to think of some feature that makes what you offer different from the competition. You may find that offering some discount or a free initial trial is enough to get you coverage.

47

UTILISING CONTINUITY OR BREAKS

Many marketing experts support the view that continuity is an essential part of any successful campaign. Instead of advertising for one week in a local newspaper, you are likely to get a better response if you continue to advertise for a number of weeks.

This takes into account the cumulative effect of your advert. If a potential client sees your advert on the first week they may well not follow it through, although a seed will have been planted. If they then see it a second week, that seed may have grown sufficiently to convince them to telephone. For other potential clients it may take three, four weeks or more.

From this you may conclude that to have a regular weekly presence must be the best approach. Logic seems to support this view, as some readers do not buy the newspaper every week and others will not see the advert in the first few weeks. Certainly some therapists confirm that booking space for a year not only works very well for them but also gives them the added advantage of being able to negotiate a large discount.

On the other hand, breaks in your advertising can also help convince potential clients that they need to take action. Some readers will have seen your advert in the newspaper every week. They may feel that they could benefit from your service but because they see your advert every week, they don't feel the need to do it now. If you stopped advertising for a few weeks, there would be some people who would then be annoyed that they hadn't written down your number or cut the advert out. They would come to the decision that if they ever saw your advert again, they would definitely follow it through. A few weeks later when your advert reappeared, the break would encourage them to take immediate action.

So both strategies can work quite successfully for you. The added advantage of booking smaller blocks of advertising space, say five weeks, is that the initial outlay is not so great and you get a chance to change newspapers if the response is poor.

48

WRITING ARTICLES

How would you like to promote your business for free in a way that gets you the kind of impact that would usually cost you hundreds if not thousands of pounds? Newspapers, particularly local newspapers, find it difficult to fill all the space they have available. They are always looking for local stories that are of interest to their readership.

This is where you can help them and yourself. Write an article which promotes your business. The article must be topical and unusual in order to be accepted. Despite all that available space, the editor won't publish just anything.

If you buy the local paper regularly you will get a flavour of the type of story they like. You can include a charity connection about helping the local community. Once you get into the right frame of mind, many, many ideas can be formulated. For instance, a headline could be:

Local Indian Head Masseur Helps Fire Brigade Relax Between Calls

Another could be:

Stop Smoking Evening Raises Funds for Local School

Ideas to help you

Ask yourself:

Q. What are the benefits of my therapy?
A. E.g. stress reduction, memory enhancement, confidence boosting.

Q. What groups of people could benefit from these?
A. Stress reduction – emergency services
    Memory enhancement – students
    Confidence boosting – job seekers

Q. Who do I need to approach to set this up?
A. Local Fire Brigade
    Police station
    Schools, colleges
    Employment office

Managing the session

1. Offer your time free to these organisations, but set limits.
2. If possible try to do a group session.
3. If you can't do group sessions give 15-minute taster sessions.
4. Ensure the group you help understands that part of the arrangement is to allow the local newspaper to run a feature on the session.
5. Give the newspaper at least one week's notice, more if possible. Be aware of their deadlines.
6. Get your practice name, address and telephone number incorporated into the article.
7. Include other ailments and problems that your therapy can help.
8. Take a supply of your brochures and business cards with you.
9. Carry your appointments diary with you.

49

RUNNING COMPETITIONS

People love to enter competitions. Look through any magazine or newspaper, national or local, and you will find a number of them. The prizes can range from a holiday for two in Mauritius to a £20 discount voucher at Marks & Spencer.

Here is your chance to gain some free publicity at the expense of providing a prize. The exposure should more than compensate for any cost you incur. In reality it is easier to place your competition in a local newspaper. They will love the idea because you are filling their space and are giving something to the readers.

You usually get the chance to write your own article with a competition. This gives you a great and cost-effective way of publicising your practice. Do not go mad and give away too much. Even if you only give away four sessions of treatment, by the time the last person, (number 4) has arrived, you will start to begrudge the free treatment you are giving. It would be better to give no more than two treatments and if possible, only one.

The usual wording is something like:

The *Stanthorpe Times* has teamed up with the Freedom Therapy Practice to offer you the chance to win a free Aromatherapy massage.

Go on to mention the different types of treatment you offer and their benefits. In addition, consider including a discount coupon for those who book a session by a certain date. Include a 'Use by' date on the coupon.

In a feature this might be written as:

'And that's not all! The *Stanthorpe Times* has negotiated a special £5 discount off any treatment offered at the Freedom Therapy Practice for our readers. So everyone can be a winner now!'

Include a contact telephone number and possibly the address of the practice. You may receive clients who don't use the coupon but book a session and pay the full amount. Either way, you are getting your practice known and this type of exposure would ordinarily cost you several times what you lose on the free session and discount coupons.

ADVERTISING PLUS!

Beware, ineffective advertising can be one of the biggest drains on your finances. Research and test the advertising medium thoroughly before committing yourself.

Connecting With Organisations

Joining forces with established bodies can give you access to many new markets for very little expense.

Marketing does not have to be a lone venture. In fact by combining with other organisations and groups you can help them achieve their aims and achieve your own marketing goals.

With joint ventures the main expense you will incur is your time. More often than not this proves to be an effective use of this valuable resource.

50

SUPPORTING NATIONAL DAYS

As well as official national holidays like Christmas, New Year, Easter and bank holidays, there is a whole host of other days, even weeks, in which to promote different messages.

Examples of national awareness campaigns

- National Stop Smoking Day
- Heart Disease Awareness Day
- Cancer Awareness Week

- Stress Awareness Day

- Save the Children Week

- National Phobia Week

Many organisations have adopted a date during the year when they get a chance to focus the public's attention on their issue. National and local newspapers, television and radio will usually give editorial space to these dates to raise awareness.

If you have advance warning of these particular days they can be a great opportunity for your practice. If you can offer a treatment to assist with an ailment or issue relevant to the national day, then you are likely to gain free publicity for yourself. Just approach your friendly newspaper editor and offer them an article that has a direct connection to the day and what you can do to help. You may get a feature without having to do anything else. However, you are more likely to succeed if you offer some form of free treatment or trial.

Connecting your therapy to national campaigns

- Polarity therapist – arrange a free energy balancing session for local nurses.

- Acupuncturist – offer 10-minute sessions to people with phobias.

- Nutritionist – provide a mini-workshop for people with high cholesterol levels.

- Colour healer – manage a group session for cancer sufferers at the local hospice.

Look at the benefits your therapy offers and match those benefits with the issue that the national date is highlighting.

51

ASSISTING AILMENT GROUPS

There are numerous organisations that offer help to individuals who suffer from a particular ailment. When conventional medicine appears to be unable to provide successful treatment, people naturally look to other means. Some motivated individuals start to put together a data bank of useful tips and tried and trusted remedies and then make this information available to others. From these humble beginnings many essential societies and support groups have started and they often go on to gain national status.

Within these organisations are people who are open to alternative treatments. They may even be more aware of how your therapy can help their particular ailment than you are. You can make contact with the national body if one exists or contact the local support group directly. A quick trip to your local library will arm you with a large number of these groups' details.

Examples of local and national groups

■ Phobics Anonymous

■ Victim Support

■ Arthritis Care

■ ME Support Groups

■ Breathe Easy Asthma Groups

■ MS Support

Approaching groups

1. Telephone the group organiser and introduce yourself then:
   – talk about the ailment, using appropriate language;
   – mention past successful cases if you can;
   – describe the benefits your therapy provides.

(This approach tends to be more successful than writing a formal letter and allows you to build a good relationship with the organiser.)

2. Volunteer your services for free initially until some trust is built up and results are seen.

3. After a trial period, ask for minimum donations to cover your time and costs.

As a volunteer therapist you may want to start your initial therapy with a group session. If, however, you can only deal with individuals, you could organise 10- or 15-minute sessions for those who are not familiar with your therapy.

Through this marketing method you can gain a reputation for helping people with a particular ailment and can legitimately say you specialise in this area. It also looks good on your CV if you apply for a paid position at a clinic. You can gain greater exposure through the support group's internal communications, such as their newsletters. Local newspapers and national dailies may be interested in running an article on 'Reflexology and How it Helps MS Sufferers' or 'How Aromatherapy Eases Asthma Symptoms', for example.

From the expertise you gain in this area, you can organise workshops to train other therapists with the methods you have found to be most successful. Members of the groups may also want to secure your services at your private practice and will be willing to pay your normal rate.

52

SUPPORTING A CHARITY

Wouldn't it be great if you were able to raise funds for your favourite local charity and add another dimension to your marketing? It would seem like one of those wonderful but rare situations where everybody wins. Yet it is quite possible to organise this.

Managing the arrangement

1. Write in the first instance to your chosen charity.
    - Offer to provide therapy for a special 'one-off' event.
    - Agree a nominal client fee (e.g. £10) which will go to the charity.
    - Use the AIDA principles described on pages 81–2, to persuade the charity that your event would be a success.
2. Follow up your letter with a phonecall a week later if necessary.
3. Make use of the charity's organisational ability and get them:
    - to take responsibility for securing a venue;
    - to set up the facilities such as a stand or room (local sports centres or shopping centres have plenty of passing trade).
4. Ensure that the charity informs all the local newspapers, radio and television stations about the event.

At face value it seems that you are giving away your time and expertise for no return. However, you will get much more back. You get free publicity for you, your therapy and your practice through the press coverage. It is vitally important to get your practice details and the ailments you can help with mentioned in the newspaper article. Every person who takes up the offer of a £10 session gives you a captive audience. Give them one of your practice leaflets and tell them how much more you can accomplish in a full session. Talk about some anonymous case histories.

Getting more from the event

1. Offer a discount on any session that is booked on the day of the event.
2. Have your diary with you, as some people will want to book straight away and you want to capture them while they are still receptive to the idea.
3. Arrange a noticeboard showing the ailments and conditions you can help with. This makes it easier for passing trade to find out more about you.

4. Have the name of your practice and a contact telephone number clearly visible.

5. Persuade someone to hand out your practice brochures to everyone passing. Make sure you have plenty of these printed, as you will need them.

Once you have decided to make this offer, your commitment must be 100%. Throw every marketing tool you can into the ring and convince everyone that they will feel better for having your therapy.

53

SPEAKING TO SOCIAL GROUPS

Social meetings and gatherings, including men's and women's clubs, are always looking for new and interesting speakers. It can be an endless nightmare for the organisers of such groups to continually have to come up with new ideas, speakers and places to visit. The members want to be entertained and enjoy their membership. Here is another win–win situation where you satisfy their requirement for a guest speaker and you find more clients.

Go to your local library and find out the names and addresses of all the social groups within a reasonable travelling distance of the venue. Then telephone one of the organisers, have an informal chat or write to them telling them what you do. Tell them you are available as a guest speaker and are willing to come along and give free demonstrations or provide a group session.

Managing your speaking engagement

1. Have your speech prepared.
2. Know your subject inside-out.
3. Consider any equipment you will need.
4. Be punctual and stick to your allotted time.

5. Keep it light and fun if possible. Don't get bogged down in technical jargon.

6. Have a few anecdotes ready to tell.

7. If you can, include some practical demonstrations.

8. Always ask for questions at the end of your speech. It gets people to think about how they would like to be helped by your therapy.

9. Have plenty of brochures with you.

At the end of your talk don't be in too much of a hurry to leave. There will always be people who will want to have a private word with you about their issue. Bring your diary with you so that you can take bookings.

Typical groups to approach

- Women's Institute

- Townswomen's Guild

- Lions Clubs

- Rotary Clubs

- Rotaract Clubs

- Amateur Dramatic Societies

- Over 50s/60s clubs

- Pensioners' social groups

- Hospital League of Friends

54

HELPING RELIGIOUS CONNECTIONS

If you are of a particular faith why not let those in your community know about your skills? Most religious groups will want to know of ways of finding extra funding for numerous projects. If you can help them in any way you will get their co-operation, which in turn can help you to attract more clients.

Given permission, you could make use of a noticeboard in your place of worship. You increase your chances of getting agreement if you donate part of your fees to the organisation. Many religious organisations organise a fete or fair to raise funds for certain causes. Use your skills to help these causes by providing taster sessions and donating your fees during these events, and you increase your standing in the community! This can gain you free local publicity.

Another way to attract clients through your place of worship is to offer discounts to fellow members. Don't expect to be inundated with clients but you might increase the possibilities of gaining more business by doing this.

Within any national or local religious group, there will always be smaller organisations that take responsibility for different matters. You will find newspapers being produced weekly or monthly, as well as many newsletters. There may be a restoration fund committee and a special appeals committee and many others all trying to raise funds.

Generally it helps if you belong to the group and are a regular worshipper, but don't let this stop you from approaching any other religious group with an offer.

55

DOING VOLUNTEER WORK

A way of cutting your teeth and gaining experience in a particular area of the community is volunteer work. During your slackest day for private clients, offer your services to a local organisation. This can be a support group for the homeless or a drop-in centre for people who are HIV positive or indeed any organisation whose cause you would like to support.

Approach the organisation as a volunteer therapist. This is the way many new therapists develop their skills quickly in their field and gain experience of a particular issue. As they progress, the issue may even become their area of expertise. Although you should not expect to be paid, some organisations will pay you a nominal fee or cover your travelling expenses.

The organisation should provide the room that you will use and, because you are a resident therapist, will normally allow you to place your leaflets and posters about their building. You will also find that you are mentioned in articles in their newsletter.

The organisation might even want to inform the local media that they can now offer your kind of therapy. This encourages more users to attend and other therapists to volunteer their services. You gain free publicity and get the opportunity to network with the other therapists. This helps reduce the isolation often felt by therapists. Effective organisations will invite you to attend an induction course to acquaint you with their procedures and give you more background about their particular issue.

With this association the organisation acquires another therapy for their client group. Your knowledge of the client group and how your service can help a particular ailment expands. In addition, you may also expect a glowing reference in the future should you need one!

56

DEALING WITH TELESALES CALLERS

If you have taken out advertising in *Yellow Pages* or elsewhere, companies will telephone you and attempt to sell you their services. Many of these telesales calls will be from companies wanting to sell client-generating promotion schemes. Be careful or you could find yourself with an increase in expenses but little in the way of new clients.

The telesales staff have been trained with a particular sales patter to convince you of all the benefits of their scheme. They will make it seem almost impossible not to be successful and imply that if you don't grab this opportunity first, your rival will. Don't be fooled! If it is that good, they will still be around next year.

Some companies play on your generosity or your guilt. They will be working on behalf of a charity and want you to take out an advert in a calendar or information brochure, for example. They won't directly ask for money, but very craftily ask for your support. They will use words like, 'Will you support the poor people in your community?' It is very difficult to say no, but if you want to stop yourself becoming poor as well and losing your business, you must! Tell them that you have your own charities that you support and that your marketing budget has been used. Only take them up on their offer if you do genuinely want to support some disadvantaged group this way. Just don't expect this to achieve any worthwhile response.

Remember, you do not have to say yes to every advertising opportunity, even though you may be pressured into meeting some artificial deadline. Insist on seeing the product you may be advertising in and always negotiate a better rate than the one you are initially quoted.

57

WORKING WITH DRIVING SCHOOLS

Look through your local telephone directory and you will find many driving schools listed. Some schools are national organisations and others are just a 'one man band'. Whatever size of school, they all occasionally have pupils whose nerves get the better of them. Their driving ability might be perfectly acceptable but on the day of the test their nervousness means that they make mistakes and fail.

The driving instructor has done all that they can as far as passing on the skills which are required to drive the car. What they often are unable to do is help those students who have a problem with their nerves and lack confidence. Such students provide opportunities for you.

Some therapies such as hypnotherapy and NLP are more adept at helping in this area, but virtually all types of therapy offer directly or indirectly a form of relaxation. If you couple your therapy with some visualisation exercises you will help any client to reduce their nervousness and feel calmer. There is no doubt that when we feel calm, we feel more in control of ourselves and confident.

Write to driving schools and tell them that you offer a programme to help nervous student drivers. Enclose a couple of business cards. If you can, show quotes from past clients as testimonials to the effectiveness of your therapy skills. Not only do you give yourself the chance of gaining referrals from driving schools but, if you include one of your leaflets with the letter, you may get the instructor along for his nerves or backache.

Becoming a qualified driver also involves passing a written examination. For a few people the practical side of driving is easy but the written paper can be daunting. Some people will remember school days and how badly they did in their history or English papers, for example. If you have experience of working with any college students and helping them with their memory and recall abilities, you can use the same process with driving school pupils. Again, include details of feedback from past relevant client successes in your letter.

CONNECTING WITH ORGANISATIONS

Even the smallest business can join forces with the largest national and international organisations to mutual benefit.

Creating Health Contacts Plus!

Any link that you can establish to orthodox health and other essential professions will bring many benefits, including enhancing clients' perceptions of trust and integrity.

As the description 'complementary therapy' implies, the treatment of any ailment or issue by a therapist (e.g. reflexologist, iridiologist, etc.) can be supportive of what is currently considered conventional medical treatment. In other words a client or patient can benefit from complementary therapies while also receiving medical help via a doctor or hospital.

A general goal of any therapist will be to seek ways of educating the medical profession by using any opportunity to prove the efficacy of complementary therapy.

The tips in this chapter not only help the therapist's marketing efforts but can also produce opportunities for bringing their service to the attention of doctors, nurses and other medical professionals.

58

ADVERTISING IN HOSPITALS

A place that the general public may frequently visit is a hospital. People go there for their own medical problems, with someone else who needs to attend for treatment or because they are visiting a friend or relative who is a patient. Whatever the reason, many people pass through a hospital's doors.

You can promote your practice in an environment where people's minds are going to be focused on their health. Just imagine a man who suffers with high blood pressure who is sitting in the patients' arrivals area and waiting to be called. He is wondering whether his blood pressure is going to improve or not. He may be on medication. He may have the opinion that medication is the only means of help, even with its side effects. Then he spots a poster offering a treatment that can help him to reduce his anxiety levels and to relax more. He might not take any action the first time he sees that poster, or the second, but at some point he will be tempted to find out more.

Likewise, outpatients who suffer with circulatory problems or breathing disorders are told that they must stop smoking. Despite this advice, many still carry on because they don't feel that they can stop without help. Then they notice some 'Stop smoking' leaflets describing a service that can help them. There is a good chance that they will at least take the leaflet away with them and telephone you for more information.

In those hospital waiting rooms you have a captive audience. Those people are bored and are looking for things to occupy their minds. They are also anxious about their ailment. If your therapy can genuinely offer them hope, you will increase your chances of turning them into a client.

Places to distribute your leaflets

■ Blood testing department

■ X-ray

■ Maternity wards and clinics

■ Accident and Emergency departments

■ Canteen and coffee areas

■ Retail outlets

■ Nurses' quarters

■ Waiting areas

Go back to the hospitals on a regular basis to check on the posters you have put up on noticeboards and the leaflets you have distributed. You will probably need to replenish the supply of leaflets every two or three weeks.

59

WORKING WITH THE EMERGENCY SERVICES

People who work for the emergency services are in the front line. Their roles involve dealing with horror, shock, violence or the results of violence. At some point in time, it takes its toll and these people can start to suffer from the effects of stress, which can reduce their ability to perform.

In any locality there are the fire services, ambulance services, and police departments. It would be rare to find an emergency service organisation that provides adequate support in the form of stress relief. The help tends to come only when someone has passed a point of no return.

Be proactive and offer your therapy to the local fire brigade. Arrange a couple of hours for a group therapy session or for short individual sessions. Involve the local newspaper to get free publicity, particularly if you are giving your services free. If the people you treat feel positive benefits, you can give them the opportunity to see you privately or give regular fortnightly or monthly group sessions. Charge a nominal fee per attendee for group sessions.

Managing your emergency services association

1. Make your service as easy as possible for them to use.
2. Get into the habit of always attending at the same time on the same weekday.
3. Get permission to put posters up in the building describing your therapy service.

4. Tailor your practice brochure to reflect how you can help the issues affecting this group of people and distribute them.
5. Ask for an article about you and your therapy to be included in the trade union's or organisation's newsletters.

Just think how impressive the title of 'Reflexologist to the Stanhope Fire Department' would be on your career record. It can also open other doors for you as far as work with organisations is concerned and you increase your chance of personal referrals through the fire station and new clients from the initial publicity of your first visit. Once you are established at one police station or fire station you can approach others with confidence.

60

ADVERTISING ON DOCTORS' APPOINTMENT CARDS

Clients who receive regular treatment from their doctor or a nurse are given appointment cards. The cards act as a reminder of the time and date of the next appointment and also give contact details of the surgery just in case the client needs to cancel and arrange a different appointment or for other queries.

Appointment cards are therefore looked at on a number of occasions by the patient and generally the patient brings the card with them to the surgery so that the next appointment can be added to it. The management of some surgeries have realised that they can generate income if they allow other services to promote their business via the cards. The smallest surgeries have around 5,000 patients and the largest can have upwards of 20,000, so the scope for your details being read by a patient is high. You could secure a reasonably prominent advertisement on the appointment card.

You could advertise on appointment cards that are given to people who have a particular ailment. These people are attending the surgery because they want to overcome that ailment. If you can also offer help with their condition, then they are likely at least to consider seeing you.

110

At first glance, it seems that this form of marketing could be quite rewarding. However, do be careful and do not sign up for just *any* price. Remember that not all of the 20,000 patients will be given an appointment card, particularly if their visit is a 'one-off'. Many patients will not be able to afford your fee, which in part is why they are seeing their doctor for help. Finally, if they are already receiving treatment they might wait to see if the conventional treatment has an effect before considering anything else.

61

REGISTERING WITH THE NATIONAL HEALTH SERVICE

Registering with the National Health Service (NHS) can add a perceived quality to your practice. Let it be clear that this does not signify any form of recognition by the NHS on the quality of your skills or your qualifications. The purpose of this registration, which involves being issued with an NHS number, is that you can obtain payment from the NHS for referred NHS patients.

This sounds as if all you have to do is accept any person who cannot afford to pay your fees as an NHS patient. In reality this is far from the truth. If the NHS is going to pay for a patient's treatment, they must be referred to you by their doctor. Even this is not enough because although the doctor might agree, the ultimate decision is made by whoever controls the NHS funds for the area. A doctor has to apply for funds to the local Health Trust. Only if the local trust agrees to pay for treatment will you be able to have the patient's treatment funded by the NHS.

These referrals tend to be few and far between, particularly because many doctors remain uninformed about complementary therapies. However, registration with the NHS is free and seems to bring with it credibility from the client's point of view. A client who notices the phrase, 'NHS Provider Number G12345' on your brochure is more likely to trust your skills.

A similar situation exists regarding funding of complementary therapies through private health companies. In practice you can register with the private health companies. However, only patients who are referred to you by a company consultant will have their treatment paid by the health company. Clients who approach you directly and have private health care will not be able to get their treatment paid for just because you are registered. But again, stating that you have a private health company provider number adds to the kudos of your practice without costing you anything, as registration is free.

CREATING HEALTH CONTACTS PLUS!

Building professional relationships with the emergency services and local and national medical bodies (doctors' surgeries, hospitals, clinics) can bring many and varied benefits to the practice of any individual therapist.

Utilising Networks

People are a therapist's most important resource, not only in terms of becoming customers but also in terms of marketing or spreading the word.

It has been said that we are never more than 6 people away from a connection to anyone in the world. Whether you believe this or not there is no doubt that through our contacts: friends, relatives, neighbours, work colleagues and acquaintances and their contacts, our potential to network is enormous. These connections are an invaluable and cost effective means of increasing your client base.

62

CREATING A 'BOARD OF ADVISORS'

Running your own business successfully often means using all the resources that you can get hold of without incurring unnecessary expense. In keeping with the expression, 'Two brains are better than one' there is a way of taking advantage of this fact without going into partnership with anyone else.

Inviting active contributors

Invite about six friends, relatives or acquaintances to a dinner party at your home. Make it clear why you are inviting them and what you expect from them. In effect, you are paying for their ideas for your business by providing them with a free dinner.

Tell them that there will be other people at the dinner (whom they may or may not know) and you just want them to contribute some ideas to help your business. The majority of people invited will be flattered to think that you hold their opinions and ideas in such high esteem. This must be true, of course, because otherwise you wouldn't have invited them.

You must do your homework before inviting just anybody. You need your guests to be as productive as possible, so invite people who you really believe will make a useful contribution and not just those who are good company socially. Also, be clear about the areas of your business that you want them to focus on. Don't let them wander off the point.

Keeping the meeting focused

If the main thrust of the evening is going to be how to increase the number of marketing strategies you use, then let them know in advance. When they arrive at the party they will then have already given it some prior thought. When the ideas start flowing, make a note of them. Don't leave them to memory.

If this function turns out well, then repeat it every few months or so. If some guests did not perform very well, replace them at the next meeting. The advantage of this informal get together is that you are not offering anyone a position in your business. It is also easy for you to change guests at your whim. It can be good, of course, to have fresh blood anyway and not always invite the same people each time.

The cost to you is the food and drink you provide plus your time. The return is the benefit of having your own 'board of advisors' or think tank all focussing on advancing your business. You also gain contacts. Someone will always say something like, 'I know someone who's looking for a therapist who can help with . . .'. Encourage them all to take away business cards to pass on to anyone who is interested in your services.

Increasing your network

At these meetings take the time to find out about the clubs and societies people belong to and whether they would like you to give a talk about your therapy or whether they have a newsletter or bulletin board that you can advertise with. It is said that we all know approximately 200 people. By tapping into your board of advisors' contacts you increase your network several fold.

63

FORMING A CO-OPERATIVE

Once a therapist has qualified and starts their practice, they will at some point start to feel isolated. This can be especially true if their previous career involved working for an organisation where they were part of a team. The usual camaraderie is no longer there; they are now the sole worker relying on their own decisions and opinions.

Reducing isolation

You can add to your marketing strategies armoury and help reduce feelings of isolation by forming a loose co-operative or network of therapists. The therapists can have different skills or offer a different type of service. For instance, in a co-operative you could have a homeopathist, herbalist, rolfer, NLP therapist, acupuncturist, reflexologist and others. No member should offer the same therapy as another. In other words, you would not have two aromatherapists because any referrals would have to be split between them.

The idea is that each therapist can refer their clients or potential clients to any of the therapists in the co-operative. Sometimes a client seeking help with a particular issue will telephone a therapist and want a personal recommendation for another form of treatment rather than picking anyone at random from the phone book. A crystal healer might refer an existing client or enquirer to the osteopath in the co-operative and truthfully assure the client that they know the therapist personally.

Forming *your* co-operative

To start the co-operative, simply look for advertisements or leaflets from local therapists and when you are ready, invite them to an informal meeting over a coffee. They will love the idea because there is no rivalry within the co-operative as no two therapists offer the same service. Meeting on a regular basis can help with reducing the isolation and is a great time to exchange ideas or plan other ventures together.

As long as everyone agrees, it can be supportive of this venture to have a supply of brochures from each member on display in all the individual practices, or at least a supply available to give to any interested client.

A client who has come to you for therapy through a personal recommendation is more trusting of you and will have more belief in your therapy skills. They will also feel safer and more secure in your practice because you are known to other practitioners and are not someone who has set up overnight.

64

JOINING AN ASSOCIATION

Any therapist who takes their profession seriously should belong to an appropriate association. The association gives credibility to its members by stipulating that they have to be of a certain standard and must abide by a code of conduct. Any membership fees should be more than offset by the benefits you gain by belonging to an association. One of those benefits can be client referrals.

The number of client referrals you receive this way can vary dramatically. Some associations actively promote themselves in such places as every edition of *Yellow Pages*. Any client who contacts them will be given details of the members in their area. Some associations have a separate marketing programme that you can join but for which you may have to pay an additional fee.

Whatever scheme your association uses you should expect at least an occasional client to be referred to you. You help this possibility by keeping in touch with the administrators of the membership. If they know your name and have spoken to you, they are more likely to suggest to an enquirer that you can help them.

Another way in which an association can help is by providing the opportunity for shared advertising. Therapists who belong to the organisation and are in the same geographical location can divide the expense of a *Yellow Pages* advertisement between them. The advert lists details of all the participating therapists (including names, designations and contact details) and states that they all are members of the association. This stated relationship between therapist and association seems to increase the perception of professionalism and trust among the general public.

Many therapists return to their associations to seek their help when they want to run a workshop for other therapists. Often the association will allow its mailing list to be used to advertise the workshop and may even sponsor the event in some capacity.

Some therapists take out membership with several associations because the fees are more than covered by the benefits they receive.

65

BUILDING NETWORKS

If you use an accountant for bookkeeping and a lawyer for legal matters, make them a part of your network. They know your success gives them opportunity for more business from you. Supply them with a few business cards and encourage them to give you referrals. This works both ways, as you can give them referrals, particularly as you are likely to mix with other small business entrepreneurs.

More networking opportunities

How many other professional contacts do you have? When a plumber comes to fix your boiler, take his card and give him your business card. While you are waiting for him to do his job, tell him about your work and all the ailments you help with and the benefits your therapy provides. Do not assume that just because he has heard of your type of therapy he knows all about it. You can do the same with the post woman or the gas meter reader or any other service provider you come into contact with. These workers mix with the general public all the time and are bound to talk about you and your therapy because it is unusual.

Talk to the cashier at the bank and at the supermarket checkout. Pass pleasantries at the hardware store and at the bakers. Drop into the conversation what you do. When you tell people that you are a therapist they become immediately interested because it is still relatively unusual. Try to plant a seed in their mind by saying as you leave, 'Well, I must be going. If you know anyone who needs a massage, just send them to me.' There is a good possibility that the next time you see this person, they will say that they have been talking about you and their friend/ relative/customer wants to come and see you. If you haven't already done so, now is your chance to give them a business card or six!

The cost to you is spending a few moments chatting. The rewards can be a regular flow of referrals.

Joining networking organisations

There are organisations that provide a more professional approach to networking. This involves paying an annual fee and meeting once a week. The meeting is usually for breakfast, for which there is another cost. The occasion involves participants making a two-minute speech about their service. Every member is encouraged to gain referrals for all other members. All referrals are monitored to see who has not only been getting referrals, but generating them. If you decide to join an organisation like this, you must commit yourself wholeheartedly to the process of selling yourself to fellow members and generating referrals to make the cost worthwhile.

66

USING MAILING LISTS

Marketing is about letting people know that you exist and persuading them that you can help with their problem or ailment. Many marketing methods use a scattergun approach. This means that for every 10 people you reach with your message, only three will need your service. Much of your effort can be wasted on those who do not need you (at least not immediately) if you are not careful.

Focusing your efforts

Using a mailing list can provide a target to aim for. Mailing lists are being constructed all the time with information about people's habits, lifestyles, likes and dislikes. Computer databases can allow for such complex manipulation of data nowadays so that if you were only interested in contacting blue-eyed, bearded men who play sport, then a mailing list could be produced for you. Every item that we buy indicates something about us and this information can be used to target us with offers of similar goods.

If a dietician wanted to attract overweight clients, a list of names and addresses could be purchased through a mailing list bureau. People who have back problems could be approached by a practitioner of the Alexander Technique. Special offers could be sent to stress sufferers with a discount on a meditation course to help them relax more.

Once a mailing list has been purchased, you can then periodically send out details of your therapy. Gift vouchers, group sessions or special offers can be communicated in this way.

Using the above approach, you can be reasonably confident that you are tapping into a warm market. (A 'warm' market is when people have indicated that they have a need for your type of service.)

If you use this strategy, be clear about the type of person you are looking for. Try to have the mailing list as focused as you can make it. Remember, your geographical location is an important factor. It is no good setting up in Colchester and getting an address for someone in Glasgow if they need to attend your practice. Purchasing mailing lists can be quite expensive. Have a clear idea on the sort of return that you require to make it worthwhile.

67

BUILDING A DATABASE

Instead of buying a list of names and addresses to promote your therapy you could build your own client database. Once a person has sampled your therapy skills, even though they may not book another session it does not mean that they will never want your services again. Often it is the case that their lives are so busy that they never get round to contacting you again. They may even lose your address and telephone details. How many times have you accepted somebody's business card, only to discover it is missing when you need it?

Reminding clients about you

Mailing an occasional promotion to previous clients who have not visited you for a while can reap rewards. Your letter can often arrive at an appropriate time and many people may see your letter as fate or perhaps they have been intending to come for therapy again. Now that they have your details once more they have the opportunity to take up the offer or even pass it on to a friend.

You can even try the old marketing ploy of giving a time-limited discount to encourage them to take action now. This can be something like:

Book your session before 31 March to receive a free
product sample or 10% discount.

You can also use your database to keep private clients informed of any classes or workshops you intend to run. Likewise people who have attended one workshop of yours should be notified of any new workshops you intend running.

This strategy will not be appropriate to every therapy. Psychotherapists, counsellors and hypnotherapists may feel that it is not ethical to approach past clients in this way, but for other therapists it may be quite acceptable.

If you build a database make sure you comply with the Data Protection Act.

68

JOINING LOCAL TRADING SCHEMES

There are a number of schemes that act like a network and encourage a form of bartering. In the UK there is a scheme called LETS (Local Enterprise Trading Scheme). This allows people who are members to trade goods and services using a fictitious currency called 'beams' (or another suitable name). Instead of hard cash changing hands, these 'beams' are used to pay for items.

The scheme helps people to offer goods for sale, skills, therapies and other commodities and their reward is to be paid an agreed amount of beams. They can in turn use the beams to purchase whatever they want from other members.

This doesn't help to pay your bills but it can save you money because in effect you are bartering your therapies for items you want. A newly-qualified therapist might need a website for promotion purposes. The therapist offers their therapy to members for a set number of beams. Those beams can then be used to hire a web designer who is also a member of the scheme. Each person decides how many beams they will charge for their services or goods.

All the LETS groups publish a newsletter at least once every three months and just like other newsletters are always looking for interesting articles. When you first join a LETS group, or even if you are a longstanding member, take the opportunity to promote your therapy by writing an interesting article. Give some tips about stress relief or goal achievement or some simple acupressure techniques, for example. The article should then say how much more can be gained by attending a session with you.

You wouldn't want to earn all your income in beams, but it is another useful way of networking.

69

EXCHANGING THERAPIES

As therapists we can appreciate the benefits of our own therapies because we see the evidence with our clients. Sometimes though, when we apply the therapy to ourselves, it can be a bit like tickling your own feet: it may not be as powerful or as enjoyable.

Exchanging therapies gains more for you

With this in mind it can be wonderful to get together with other therapists in your area and exchange therapies. You could swap an acupuncture session for a reflexology session or kinesiology session for a meditation session. The benefits of this are that you gain experience of what another therapy is like and also how another therapist works. Also, because you now know another therapist through personal experience you will feel more confident about recommending them to people, and of course they will feel able to recommend you.

It is important to be clear about your exchange, swap or barter agreement with anyone. A Reiki therapist may charge £40 per hour while a Rosen body worker may charge £60 per hour. If these two therapists decide to swap their services, is it fair to exchange an hour of therapy or should the fee differences be taken into account? Usually, for simplicity's sake a straight swap will be agreed; one session of Reiki for one session of Rosen body work.

Unlimited benefits

Exchanging does not have to limit itself to fellow therapists. You could barter your services with a bricklayer or decorator or anyone who is agreeable to such an arrangement. The more people you treat with your therapy, the greater are your chances of your reputation spreading and attracting paying clients.

70

MENTORING

I am sure most people have heard the expression 'Why re-invent the wheel?'. The lesson of this saying applies to your therapy practice in many ways. Instead of making mistakes that can cost you time, money and maybe your reputation, why not learn from someone else's mistakes?

Find someone who is a success at what they do. This person should ideally be providing the same therapy that you are skilled in and have a practice that you would like to have for yourself. In other words, they have achieved, or are well on their way to achieving, the type of thriving practice you dream of. By finding such a person, you support your confidence that your dreams can become your living reality because someone is already out there doing it. Secondly, you have found a perfect mentor.

Some successful therapists will not want to take on the responsibility of mentoring another therapist for a variety of reasons. The trick in getting someone to assume the role is not to make the 'mentor' title official. If you just ask for advice, the seasoned therapist will be happy to help because they may recall how they struggled initially and were helped by others. You should also use your mentor's time sparingly. You can still try things out for yourself and learn from your mistakes but you may want some guidance for the major decisions.

Try not to be a carbon copy of your mentor but incorporate your own style and aim to improve on your mentor's suggestions. There is, of course, nothing to stop you having more than one mentor.

UTILISING NETWORKS

Utilising networks provides many opportunities to market your therapy. Whether through 'word of mouth' or other means, use this invaluable resource as much as possible.

Using Retail Outlets

It can be very rewarding to form loose partnerships with local traders of all varieties to increase your profile.

Other local businesses that are not in direct competition with your business can prove a useful source of new clients. Retail businesses that attract a large number of people from all walks of life can be highly fertile grounds for new clients.

With the right approach most retailers will be happy to assist you with your marketing especially if they are aware of the benefits they will derive from helping you.

71

JOINING FORCES WITH HAIRDRESSERS

There is no doubt that personal recommendation is the best form of advertising for any business, not least because it is without cost. When people get together for any reason, they usually end up chatting about any subject from politics to sport, noisy neighbours to the family. Hairdresser and barber shops seem to provide an excellent environment for the passing of opinions, information and gossip not only by the customers but also by the staff.

When your hair is being cut, permed, washed or dyed there isn't a lot you can do to pass the time other than to talk. The staff realise that if they engage the customer in conversation it helps them to relax and enjoy their time there. The customer has opinions and will generally make them known. Furthermore, customers can hear other conversations and may offer a word of help or laugh with a joke.

Advice is free and most people like to pass on their 'pearls of wisdom', given the chance. The hairdresser's is also a place where people unburden themselves and start to talk about their problems.

From the therapist's point of view, this environment and the interactions that happen within its boundaries can provide a rich seam of clients. It only takes one customer to talk about your practice and suddenly many others are listening. People like to hear about the unusual and, even though complementary and alternative therapy is becoming more popular, it is still considered something outside the norm and, special. Therefore it is intriguing.

Even if a customer at the hairdresser's doesn't admit to needing help they can still be making a mental note and seek out your services at a later date.

All of the above will work as long as you have someone who talks about the therapy they received from you. Given the opportunity, they will do this, as long as their problem was not of a delicate or personal nature.

Tapping into a rich seam of clients

What can really help your marketing is if one of the hairdressers talks about your therapy. The hairdresser is in a position of influence and can be of great value to you. With this in mind, be proactive and seek their help. There are a number of tactics you can use. The direct approach of 'Will you recommend me to clients?' is unlikely to work unless they have sampled your therapy first hand.

You could offer one of the hairdressers a free session. This could be amply rewarded by any referrals. If it works out well you may even consider giving, in turn, each of the staff a free session.

Swapping a therapy session for a haircut could be another way of getting your services known. In this way you get something immediately for your services plus the prospect of referrals.

Gaining those clients

Another way is to leave some small leaflets at all the hairdressers in your locality. The manager of the establishment will, nine times out of ten, have no objection to you leaving some leaflets, particularly if you suggest they are for his or her clients. You can use wording like this:

> *'Hi, I am a local reflexologist (or aromatherapist or naturopath, etc.) . . . I just wondered whether I could leave a few leaflets for your clients?'*

You will be amazed at how the staff can become very interested in you. They don't have many therapists coming to their door and you may find yourself being quizzed about your therapy. This shows that they are interested in you. They are not being hostile. Go to as many salons as you can and don't forget your own favourite place.

Every so often call back and refresh those leaflets. Tell them that some of your new clients have found out about you through them. They will feel good about helping you and be happy to take more leaflets.

You just need to say something like:

> *'I don't know if you remember me but I am the local reflexologist who left some leaflets here last month . . . Well, I just wanted to say, thanks very much because I've been able to help some of your customers.'*

As you leave, (as an afterthought) say:

> *'Oh by the way, just in case you've run out, I thought I would drop in a few more leaflets.'*

You will find very little objection and again you leave the staff of that business feeling good about themselves.

72

MARKETING IN SHOPS

An economical way of bringing your therapy to the attention of potential clients is advertising via your local shops. In its simplest form, you write on a postcard the details of what you are offering and a contact telephone number. Then you pay by the week for the card to be displayed in the shop window.

Rates vary but are still fairly low. This form of marketing will not appeal to everyone or be appropriate to the nature of every therapy. It would probably not work for the psychotherapist as the potential client may get the impression of someone who is not qualified or has little or no experience.

Yet for an aromatherapist, a more flexible perception of what is appropriate may be enjoyed. This is particularly so if the format of the advert elevates it above the surrounding mass of hand-written advertisements. If you decide to use this method, be creative. Use a different-coloured card. Have the description typed or printed. State the benefits of your treatment and also include that you are professional, qualified and experienced. Include designations after your name to assist the air of professionalism.

Some shops will allow you to place a poster in the window. This gives you an even better chance to stand out from the run-of-the-mill – bikes, furniture and other household goods for sale or wanted. You will probably be paying more for this but it could be worthwhile.

Be choosy about which shops you pick in which to advertise. Opt for the most popular ones. You can easily spot these by watching the number of customers entering and leaving. Also watch out for the number of people who stop to read the notices in the window. Set a trial period for this option to see whether it will work for you.

73

PROMOTING ON CAFE MENUS

Cafés and smaller restaurants are places where people meet and talk on a regular basis. Families, friends and even individuals will often drop into a place to get something to eat or drink or both.

This is a chance to attract more clients and to do it in a way that builds a good relationship with local eating establishments. It will not cost you the earth and yet you can secure advertising all year round.

Spotting an opportunity

All these eating places have one thing in common – a menu. In these establishments the customers always scan the menu. Even if they know what they want, they will look through the menu just to see if there is anything else of interest. This is your opportunity to increase your profile and at little cost.

Approach the manager or owner of the café and offer to provide them with new menus once a month. By menus, I mean the sheets of paper or cardboard that detail the different dishes and not the plastic outer coating or fancy folder (if there is one). You offer to do this for the café owner for free.

Give to get

You arrange to have the menus printed (on your computer or a borrowed one). This is your cost. In return, you get to advertise your therapy on the menu. You will need to negotiate how much space you can take up. If you choose a smallish café of about 12 to 20 tables, the print costs should be no more than £5 per month. That is £5 per month to have your business benefits in front of potential customers every time that café is open.

The café owner benefits by getting clean new menus at least once a month and getting a chance to change the meals or prices or both. The owner could more easily run special meals for different seasons as well as for Easter and Christmas. The owner gets this for free as part of the agreement.

A variation on the above is to provide business cards which sit in an attractive container on each table instead of printing your practice details on the menu. This is another way of bartering services – and your printing costs can still be claimed as a legitimate business expense.

74

COMBINING WITH BEAUTY AND HEALTH SHOPS

Places where people think about how good they look and feel are a beauty parlour or health shop. These places are great for finding more paying clients.

Utilising available resources

A number of possibilities await you. Some of these establishments will have a spare room that is being under-used, if it is used at all. Approach the manager and suggest the idea of running a part-time service from that room.

The benefits for the shop are that they get some rent from your use of the room. They also get the chance to sell more of their services or products to your clients. Once the backroom is fit for use, the shop manager may invite other therapists to use it on the days that you do not.

With this arrangement, you get another place to practise and, because it is in the interest of the shop for you to succeed, they will help to get clients for you. The best arrangement (from your point of view) is to pay rent by the hour and only when you use the room. In other words, you only pay rent when you have a client. If you don't get this agreement, do think seriously about whether to walk away from this shop or not. Remember that if you pay rent whether you have clients or not, then the shop manager does not have any incentive to attract clients for you because whatever happens they still get their rent.

Increasing your chances of success

Encourage the shop owner to display your practice brochures in a good place in the shop. If you produce an A5 size leaflet giving details of your therapy, you might also persuade the shop owner to enclose one of these with items bought by the customer. If you can get permission, place a good sized poster (minimum A4) giving details of your service in the shop window. Include your own telephone number on the poster, thereby increasing your chances of gaining business even when the shop is closed.

75

CAMPAIGNING AT SHOPPING CENTRES

Whenever you plan to have a 'blitz' on marketing it is useful to consider all the places where people congregate, visit or pass through for whatever reasons. A shopping centre of any size has people passing through it every day. The busiest day is usually a Saturday.

Think back to the last time you visited such a place and remember what happened as you went from store to store. Eventually, somewhere someone would have tried to thrust something into your hand. They might have been inside the shopping complex or standing outside, but there would have been at least one person doing this – if not several.

Stop me and take one

Companies small and large do this type of marketing for a reason. It must bring in customers for them. If it works for them it can work for you. If you don't have the nerve to do it yourself, or don't want to be seen handing leaflets out, get a friend to do it or pay someone to stand there for you. It might prove to be a waste of time, but on the other hand it might be that winning strategy that you will want to use on a regular basis.

Do not use your most expensive leaflets or brochures. The majority of these will end up as rubbish. Make up an A5 size flyer from 80gsm paper and emphasise the problems you can help with. Your contact telephone number should be large but the name of your practice or your own name should be smaller. Highlight the words that attract people such as, FREE, DISCOUNT, SPECIAL OFFER, etc. If you give a free initial consultation, make sure this is mentioned and highlight benefits before features of your treatment.

Useful research

Before putting together your flyer, start to collect other flyers and see how they are designed. It will prevent elementary mistakes and enable you to make an impact the first time.

Check out the different shopping centres in your locality. Some will provide a better response than others. Make a list of those centres in the order that you feel would give you the best response. If you are going to stand inside the building you should check with the management to make sure that they have no objection to this. If you stand outside the centre on public land and hand your flyers out, there will generally be little problem.

Decide a set number of flyers to hand out at each centre and when this has been reached, move on to the next one. Depending on the distance, you may only be able to cover two or maybe three shopping centres in any one day. At each location start handing out your flyers as soon as you arrive.

Don't be put off by anyone who refuses to take a flyer or immediately throws it away. Every person you see who is not interested in your therapy means that you are that much closer to someone who is.

Don't expect the telephone to ring constantly because some people keep these flyers for months or even years before acting on them. If anyone asks you questions, do give them your time, as it shows that they – and you – are interested.

76

TEAMING UP WITH SPECIALIST SHOPS

With the popularity of 'New Age' ideas and spirituality today, you can find many shops that specialise in selling books, tapes, crystals, stones, etc. People who spend their money in these shops are likely to be more open and accepting of your therapy.

Join forces to increase success

Forming an alliance of some sort with such a shop may prove to be a very useful strategy. Sometimes these shops have noticeboards where therapists are encouraged to leave leaflets and business cards. These get swamped and so you may find the leaflet you pinned up one day is under a pile of others the next day. You will get more consistent results (new clients) from this type of shop by having a closer connection.

Use your creative skills to put together a scheme that will benefit you and the shop. That should not be difficult. If you are a crystal healer, you could offer sessions from the shop, first having agreed this, of course, with the owner/manager of the shop, for half a day a week. You get paid by the customers who are directed to you by the shop. The shop takes a percentage of your earnings for providing the space, and also earns from people who want to buy their own crystals.

You could negotiate a similar arrangement so that any customers enquiring about seeing a crystal healer will be given your business card or leaflet. Likewise, you can recommend to clients that they get their crystals from that shop. Another example of this arrangement is for an aromatherapist to team up with a shop that sells oils, candles, and incense burners.

With this arrangement, everybody wins. The customer gets what they want: the therapy. The shop gets what they want: rent from the space you use and increased sales. You get paying clients in the shop and referrals to your private practice.

77

REACHING SUPERMARKET CUSTOMERS

The larger supermarkets are offering ways for local businesses to reach local customers. Next time you do your weekly shop, have a look at the back of the receipt. You may find all different types of local businesses advertising their products and services.

Before committing yourself to this type of advertisement you will need to be clear on how well it works for those who have already used it. Telephone any company that you find on the back of a receipt and ask them. If the business is a small one, like yours, most of the time they won't mind just giving a rough idea of its success. The ultimate test of whether it is a good promotion medium is whether they will renew their contract with the supermarket.

You will also need to find out how long the contract runs for and the geographical location of the supermarkets that will use till receipts with your advert. You don't want to pay for something with a wide coverage, most of which would be of little benefit to you.

Another way of making yourself known to the throngs of people that pass through your local supermarket is to check out their customer information area. Sometimes they provide a customer noticeboard. This is where customers can place notices to sell unwanted items or state what they are looking for. It can also be a place for you to display a small notice about your therapy.

Some supermarkets and some large hardware chains are providing a business card dispenser service. This is simply a facility for local businesses to provide a supply of business cards for customers to take. There is a charge for this service. You can choose to go in one store, or a number of them, in your location. It is better to try one store at a time to gauge the likely success of this medium. The position of the dispenser is very important. People are naturally lazy and won't go out of their way to look at it. Check those in your local stores and pick a store where virtually all customers pass by the dispenser. One of the better positions is after customers have paid for their goods and as they are leaving the store.

78

WORKING IN A CAFE

Local cafés need to attract a regular clientele as well as passing trade. As with other establishments, it is the regular customers that keep a business healthy. A café needs to persuade customers that not only are their coffees, cappuccinos and other beverages superior to those that you could make at home but that there are other benefits. Rather than being a place just to drink coffee and chat with friends, some cafés are extending their attractiveness.

More than just coffee

Lately, coffee and computers have come together to form internet cafés. With bookshops now offering fresh coffee, some cafés are turning the tables and displaying a range of books for sale that customers can browse through at their leisure while enjoying their coffee.

You can assume that café owners are open to new and exciting additions to their service. Here is an opportunity for the creative therapist. What service could you offer to the cafe's customers?

Any therapy you propose for this environment needs to take into account that it is a public place and privacy cannot be assured. There will usually be limited space in a cafe, so your therapy must not take up much room, or be disruptive to customers who just want to enjoy a chat and a coffee.

Ideas for therapists

- Reflexologist – could work on people's hands rather than their feet.

- Massage therapist – could provide Indian head massage.

- Nutritionist – could advise on suitable vitamins and minerals.

- Crystal therapist – could offer a re-balancing service.

Give a flavour only

All of the above should be short versions of the full therapy. Your aim is to give a flavour of the therapy and not a full session. You can charge a nominal amount for a short session. The cost should be small enough to allow customers to make an easy decision to buy and large enough to make it worth your while. If you build up a good relationship with the café owner before you propose any of the above services, you should be able to negotiate a fair agreement for your use of the café. Some café owners recognise that you are making the café a more attractive place and that word of mouth will bring more customers in. These customers will spend their money in the café and so you may not be charged anything for your use of one table.

To build a regular clientele and to let new clients find you, it is best to have a set day and time that you will make yourself available at the café. Negotiate to have a notice put up in the café window publicising your service. Always bring plenty of brochures and business cards and your appointment diary with you.

USING RETAIL OUTLETS

Use your creativity to invent schemes that enable you to team up with other local businesses for mutual benefits.

Using the Internet and Social Media

The internet is constantly changing. The long-term successful therapist keeps up to date with changes in any areas that can affect their practice in a positive or negative way.

You must set up your own website because one thing is for sure – your competitors have already done this. A website is now a vital part of a successful marketing strategy. Without a website, you will be viewed as outdated and potential customers may perceive the therapy you offer as outdated too.

79

SETTING UP A WEBSITE

There are many ways of putting together a website that even the complete novice can tackle. Many therapists barter their services for something they want. Usually you will find someone in your circle of family and friends who will be a self-taught expert on the internet and will have already put together their own website. Why not barter some of your therapy sessions to get your website built?

Alternatively you may decide to employ a web design company to put together a slick site and handle the technical details and registrations for you.

If you fancy the idea of tackling designing and programming your website there are plenty of easy-to-use software packages that can help you do this. Some website-building software can be obtained for free such as at www.nvu.com. Using NVU you can take a free website template and import it into this software and then edit it and once completed, upload it to your website hosting space. Other software such as Serif's Website plus is reasonably priced and easy to use. At the more expensive end of the market is Dreamweaver.

Other options that can also be free are at www.moonfruit.com and www.weebly.com Here the hosting is provided for you along with free templates. The downside is that your domain name will include the words moonfruit or weebly such as www.massage.moonfruit.com or www.massage.weebly.com.

Today websites are produced in many different coding languages. The original language that most websites used was HTML (HyperText Markup Language). It is useful but not crucial to have an awareness of some elements of HTML. Fortunately these elements are quite easy to understand.

Your website address or domain name

Nothing beats having a domain name that reflects the business you are in. Whereas free domain names provided by telephone companies may have been acceptable in the past, they would be regarded as a poor substitute today.

Choosing your domain name requires some careful thought. Some therapists or coaches choose to have their own name as their domain name such as www.fredsmith.com. This can work very well as you will establish your name with your service and your reputation.

The drawback about choosing your name as your website address is that you lose the advantage of including keywords. Keywords are the words a potential customer will use to find your type of service in the search engines. For a reiki practitioner an important keyword is 'reiki'. Search engines love to see keywords as part of the domain name and will give a boost to the rankings of a website that has these.

An example of a website that includes keywords would be:

www.reiki-practitioner.co.uk

The above example includes two keywords 'reiki' and 'practitioner'. This is what is termed as good SEO (Search Engine Optimisation). However, there could be quite a lot of competition for those two keywords when you realise how many reiki practitioners there are in the world. A way of helping your ranking that is more targeted to where your business is based is to include your geographical location. Customers will mostly want to find the service they seek near to their home or place of work.

Choosing a domain name that includes the type of service you offer and your location gives you added advantage in the search engine rankings. When you incorporate both these elements in your domain name an example would be:

www.reiki-practitioner-birmingham.co.uk

Don't worry if the domain name that feels the best for your business has been taken already. There is a high probability that you will still be able to secure the domain name you want by being flexible about the type of domain (e.g. .com, .co.uk, .net, etc.) you have for your chosen website address.

Usually if you are based in the UK you might choose .co.uk as the type of domain name you want. However .com domain names are so well known that many UK and other business choose .com. If the .com and .co.uk versions of your domain name have been taken then there are a raft of other options for you.

There are these types of domains to choose from including .biz, .info, .org, .org.uk, .net, .co, .eu and many more. Check with various webhosting websites to find out what is available.

It is important to make use of the email address that comes with the purchase of your domain name. Never use free email addresses as this loses you some professional perception points in the eyes of a potential client. So typically an email address that can be used with our example above would be fred@reiki-practitioner-birmingham.co.uk. Once you have an email address and a website, include these details on all your business paperwork. It provides a different way for people to contact you. Another advantage is that people can retain a sense of anonymity when emailing you and may ask questions which they don't feel comfortable with asking by telephone. This can encourage potential clients to find out more about you and reduce their fears.

Dealing with the doubters

Your site can also help with people's objections (i.e. reasons for deciding not to book your service) by having a page dedicated to frequently asked questions (referred to as 'FAQs'). Just list the top 20 questions that you get asked about your therapy and then itemise these questions with the answers on your website. This can save you a lot of time.

Designing your website

Your website must be interesting, pleasant to the eye and easy to navigate. Do not use a multitude of colours. Choose three or four colours and use them consistently. For example, choose a deep blue for the background, white text and bold yellow for headings. There is always a temptation to use too many images. Images take time to appear and will slow down the loading of your page. If a web page takes too long to display, visitors will get bored and move on to another site.

Your site must be slick (look stylish and modern), fast (load within three seconds) and to the point (informative without being boring). Moving around your site from page to page should be easy and all the obvious information should be clearly accessible. There is a term in website design circles known as being 'sticky'. This means that if you have a good site, your visitors will stick around and may even come back for more. If it is not sticky any visitor will move to another website very quickly. For most internet visitors you have less than 30 seconds to make a good impression!

There are basic sections of information that should be included on any website no matter what type of business you operate. These are:

1. Home page – this is usually the first page your web visitors will land on. It should summarise what your website is about. The first page must be uncluttered and navigation to other information should be easy and logical. If you have a lot of information to communicate on a number of sub-topics, either include a brief overview or include one paragraph and the option to read more with a link to another internal page of your website where the sub-topic is expanded upon in more detail.

2. Therapy/Coaching – this describes the therapy or type of coaching you're offering. Describe what type of service you offer and the typical issues it helps with.

3. About us – this is your page for describing your training, qualifications and experience. Any information that helps you appear different from your competitors will be worth adding here.

4. FAQs – A 'Frequently asked questions' page is essential for what are called 'objections'. Objections are just the barriers that potential customers have to booking your service. Typical FAQs will be 'How much does it cost?' and 'How many sessions will I need?'

5. Location and Booking – give details of where your business is located if your clients need to come to you. If you provide mobile therapy or coaching via the telephone or online describe how this works.

6. Contact Us – This gives clear instructions on how to book your service.

Crucially you should include on every single page of your website your location (the town or city and not necessarily the exact postal address) your contact telephone number and email address. Don't frustrate your visitors by making it hard for them to know where you are and how to get in touch with you.

On-site page optimisation

On-site optimisation refers to those elements that will help your website to rank well in the search engines that need to be included as part of your website design.

If you use website design software, you will be given the chance to add certain details to each page of your website. These details form part of the coding of your website which search engines use to allocate a rank for your website. These are not visible to human website visitors but are to the search engines.

These details, (often referred to as meta tags) are important, and need to be given some prior thought and are: the title, description and keywords for any and every page of your website. The design software will take these details and enter them into your website in the form of HTML coding (meta tags).

This is where that little bit of HTML knowledge can come in handy if you want to do this manually. To add or amend these meta tag details without any web design software, open your webpage file using free software (this usually comes with any PC) called Wordpad or Notepad.

Near the top of the page you will notice this:

<title>The title of your webpage</title>

Title

This is simply the title that you give to a web page. You should use this meta tag as another opportunity for repeating your keywords. Although search engines' algorithms (the formula they use to calculate a website's rank) change, generally, your title should have around five to eight words. The first few words should repeat your keywords. If you are a London-based herbalist the coding for this could look like:

<title>Herbalism by a London Herbalist</title>

Keywords

The meta tag to look at is called keywords. These are words that web surfers will use in search engines to describe what they want to find. The HTML coding will typically look like this:

<META name="KEYWORDS" content= "keyword1, keyword2, etc">

If you are a herbalist, some of the keywords a client may use to find you are: herbalist, herbalism, herbs. With this in mind the coding could look like this:

<META name="KEYWORDS" content= "herbalist, herbalism, herbs">

You can include as many keywords as you want within the coding above. It may be useful to include your city or town, county and country such as:

<META NAME="KEYWORDS" content= "herbalist, herbalism, herbs, London, England">

Description

This meta tag describes the content of your site. It often appears as the short description shown in the search engine rankings and looks like this.

<META NAME="DESCRIPTION" content= "This is a description of what my web page is all about">

When performing a search engine enquiry, you are usually shown the first ten websites with their web addresses (URL) and a description for each site. It is the description of a site that will encourage an internet visitor to go to that site or not. Make your description short and to the point. Include the benefits of your therapy and any USP (Unique

Selling Proposition) like a free initial consultation. The coding for a description could be:

<META NAME="DESCRIPTION" content= "Herbalism to help you resolve your problems such as fears, stress, pain, IBS and much more. Enjoy a free initial consultation from a London based Herbalist">

Including some of your keywords in your description is important and can help improve your webpage's search engine ranking.

ALT tags

One last piece of HTML coding that can be useful to be familiar with is called 'alt' tags. These relate to any images or photos on your webpage(s). If you use web design software you will probably be given the opportunity to enter this information when you position or add an image to the design of your web page. 'Alt' is an abbreviation of the word 'alternative' and gives a worded description of the image or photo. In days gone by, some people would not be able to see photos because the memory requirements were too great and would as an alternative, see the alt word description for the photo. With the advent of broadband and faster internet services this is less likely to be the case but the alt tag is still used and utilised to help your page ranking.

If you use website design software then you can ignore this next section. However if you are not sure, simply open up your webpage with Wordpad or Notepad and do a search for 'img' using Edit from menu. When you find 'img' this will refer to the code for an image. As you move along the code you will see the name of the image file such as 'image1.jpg' or 'image1.gif' (there are a number of image file extensions but .jpg and .gif are the most popular). As you keep looking at the coding you might see coding for width and height. What you are really interested in is the coding for alt. If it isn't there already you will see something like this:

<img src="home.jpg" height="150" width="150" align="right">

If you don't find any alt text in the image coding you can add it. Here is an example:

<img src="home.jpg" height="150" width="150" align="right" alt="Herbalism in London">

The important point here is that the alt text can be used to squeeze in some of your keywords and can help your search engine ranking.

Remember to make a copy of any web page files you attempt to change in this way just in case you make a mistake and need to return to the unedited version.

Is one website enough?

Most therapists and coaches have one website. However, it can be a smart move to consider, at some point in time, having two or more websites. The reason for this is partially to minimise a threat to your business and also to increase an opportunity.

A threat to any business website is that the website itself might be unavailable. This can be because your host is performing some maintenance work. Sometimes the data discs on which your website is hosted may crash and need replacing, in which case your website might be unavailable for several days. There is the possibility, no matter how remote, that your hosting company stops operating as a business, and your website will be down until you can transfer your domain to another host.

The opportunity that can be enjoyed by having another website is that each website can focus on ranking high in the search engines for different keywords. You might have two practices that are based in Birmingham and London and may be you want your location included in the domain name. Also you might have an issue that you specialise in and want to make this the core subject of a new website such as www.weight-loss-hypnosis.com.

If you decide to invest in another website, to minimise the threat mentioned above, choose a different hosting company from the one, you have for your first website.

If you are just starting out as a new business, focus on getting one website up and running first. Once that is established and performing well, only then consider adding one or more websites.

80

LISTING WITH SEARCH ENGINES AND DIRECTORIES

Having a website that gives details of your therapy is a step forward but is not the end of what you can do to promote yourself. In fact having a website will not bring in the number of client or customer enquiries that you want or need by itself. Having a website is akin to building a shop out in the countryside and away from any major town or city. The shop might have quality goods or services on offer but it lacks customers because the customers do not know that the shop is there.

On the internet, potential customers are often referred to as 'traffic'. What you need to do is to put up signs to let the traffic know where your shop is located and what it is offering. One important way that you achieve this is to get your website listed in the major search engines and in various web directories.

Potential customers use search engines and directories to find businesses like yours and in doing so create traffic to your website. Therefore you must get your website listed in the major search engines.

There are literally hundreds of search engines. You could waste a lot of time trying to get listed on every one of them. This strategy would not be as efficient as choosing to get listed on the most popular search engines.

Popular search engines

- www.yahoo.com

- www.bing.com (this is the search engine for MSN)

- www.google.com

146

All search engines provide on-line forms for you to submit your website for inclusion. However, just because you submit your website doesn't mean that it will be accepted. You will need to obey certain criteria. These will usually be stated if you decide to fill in the submission form. Some search engines offer a submission service that you have to pay for. Never use this service as 'paid for' submission does not guarantee acceptance.

Although the search engines provide submission forms, some internet marketing experts are of the opinion that it is best to let the search engines find your website by themselves. I prefer to do this too. The means by which the search engines will find your new website is via links from other websites that point at yours. Links from other websites are referred to as backlinks which are a vital element of internet marketing and are described later in this chapter.

A search engine that has acquired a special authority that other search engines respect is www.dmoz.org If you can get your website listed with dmoz it will boost your ranking in the other search engines.

Go to one of the three main search engines of Google, Bing or Yahoo, and enter a search term or keyword phrase (eg. Reiki in Birmingham). You will see 'paid for' advertisements that relate to those keywords, at the top and right-hand side, and in the middle of the results page, you will also see a list of what is referred to as 'organic rankings'.

Organic search rankings are trusted more by people who browse the internet because they know that the other listings are advertisements and have been bought by businesses. If you want your website to be found on page 1 of any search engine, you can invest in the advertising boxes at the top or right-hand side of the results displayed. In Google these are called Adwords and Yahoo and Bing have their own versions of this.

It can be worthwhile investing in this type of internet marketing but be careful. Make sure you research this opportunity well and ensure you always set a budget for your spending.

As competition increases for businesses which are chasing the same keyword phrases, the cost of being on page 1 of the search engines increases too. The cost is referred to as cost-per-click (cpc). Every time someone clicks on your advertisement, your account is charged. Getting on page 1 for the keywords 'Reiki in Birmingham' may be 50p a click. If ten people click on your advert in one day, the cost to you would be 10 x 50p = £5. You can see how your advertising budget can soon be depleted if you don't set a limit to your daily advertising spend.

Using cpc advertising can provide a quick route to getting traffic to your website as long as you know what you are doing and monitor the results of your campaign. Google, Yahoo and Bing provide extensive help facilities, including detailed statistics of your advertisement's performance to enable you to make informed decisions about the right options for your business.

Your search engine ranking

In the UK the search engine that is used more than any other is Google. The other two search engines are important too but your focus should be on gaining a good ranking in Google and you will probably find that you will rank well in the other two search engines anyway.

Once you know or suspect that your website has been listed by Google (or Yahoo or Bing) find out what ranking it has achieved. You can do this manually by visiting every page of Google for the keywords you are checking (e.g. Reiki in Birmingham) until you find it. There are various free rank checkers that you can use on-line which can make this job quicker. The drawback with these rank checkers is that they may only check a limited number of pages.

It's important to know where your website ranks for a keyword phrase as this information not only acts as a benchmark but it will motivate you to continue to use various tactics and strategies described in this chapter as you see your ranking improve.

Keyword phrases

As previously described, the inclusion of keywords in your meta and alt tags are to let the search engines know what the subject of your website is and therefore the keyword phrases that they should rank your website for.

However, if you include keywords in your meta and alt tags but never mention those keywords in the words, sentences and descriptions you display for your visitors, the search engines may doubt the importance of those keywords. This will result in your rank for those keywords not being as high as it could be. Remember that your keywords must be mentioned somewhere in the body of your website to show consistency to the search engines.

Avoid spamming

Some people who code their own websites make the mistake of packing their pages with their keywords. This is called spamming. Do not do this as this tactic can be detected by the search engines and your website's rank will be penalised for it. Also, if you pack keywords into your web pages descriptions you run the risk of making the descriptions unreadable for your web visitors and they will leave your website rapidly.

Monitoring your website ranking

Web design companies will program and publish your site and will submit them to the search engines for you. This does not guarantee that you will either be accepted by the search engines or achieve a high ranking. Taking an interest in the coding of your website and using the examples above will enable you to play an active role in achieving a better ranking and ultimately lead to more visitors to your site. Even when you have managed to appear in the top 50 websites for your keyword(s), you will still need to monitor your position and improve it. If a website's content remains the same for too long, the search engines will assume that it may not be as relevant and start to let it drop down the rankings. Keep your content fresh for the internet surfers and for the search engines and you will maintain its popularity.

81

UTILISING SOCIAL MEDIA WEBSITES

The internet is ceaselessly evolving new facilities and new forms of communication are being developed and then promoted. In recent times these websites and the facilities they offer have been termed 'social media' websites. These websites encourage you to become a member and then to encourage all your family, friends, work colleagues to join up too. The idea is that you communicate with your own community of known people and that you expand your social network by inviting other members to become your friends.

Some of the most popular websites that offer social interaction in various forms are:

- www.facebook.com

- www.myspace.com

- www.bebo.com

- www.friendster.com

- www.hi5.com

There are hundreds of other social networking websites that offer similar facilities to their members. Some have a specific subject in mind such as the photographs website www.flickr.com All want you to become members and to bring your networks to these websites.

There is an expression in marketing circles which is 'Go where the hungry crowd is'. This means that if a large number of people are congregating in a certain place, there is an opportunity for any business if they too make their presence felt there. So if potential customers are members of these social interaction websites, your business could gain new customers if you sign up as a member too.

There are two ways of marketing your business on social networking websites. One way is to pay for advertising offered by that website and the other is to do exactly what the purpose of these websites is, to join in and interact with members

Dos and Don'ts of social networking

No one likes a pushy salesperson and if you come across as that in any interactions you have with others it will be ignored. Also if you keep mentioning in every post you make with other members that you do this therapy or you provide that type of coaching and they should use your service, you will probably lose more than you gain.

To gain customers from social network sites you need to deliver a sense of value to other members. Giving value to others helps to create trust and a reputation that makes you stand out in a positive way. Giving value can be achieved in a number of ways. The easiest way is to be encouraging, positive and supportive of other members. So if someone discusses an issue or problem they have, be supportive and understanding, and then suggest some possible solutions. Don't plug your own service but if you provide for example, reflexology sessions, mention reflexology as one of your suggested solutions (if it is appropriate) among the other solutions. Don't over-egg it though. By using this gentler approach to marketing on social network websites, you will be perceived as an expert in your therapy but not someone who pushes your practice inappropriately. Remember that if you push your business too much, it will start to irritate others and they will stop reading your messages even though they might contain helpful information. Be ready to recommend services that are not connected to your business to show that you have the best intentions in mind.

You can also write articles on your area of expertise. These should be informative rather than blatant sales copy. An example of a social interaction website that allows for article writing and networking is:

www.gather.com

A vital part of networking and building a reputation is your active support for other businesses and non-business members. Most social networking sites provide a facility where you can comment or even give a rating for someone else's articles, posts, photos or other interactions. Be helpful to other businesses and members by making a habit of giving them positive feedback and a good rating and you will often find that they reciprocate. If you are unable to leave positive feedback, don't leave negative feedback as it is best not to leave any at all. You do not want to create enemies on-line and some people will take offence and seek revenge if your comments upset them. If you need to be critical, find a way of doing so which is informative and include some positive comments to provide some sense of balance. A sense of humour is a great way of building a great reputation too.

82

AUTHORING WEB ARTICLES

A proven way of gaining credibility and expert status online is to write articles. Articles that you author should be original and not plagiarised from any other source. Your articles should be both informative and easy to read. They will be aimed at potential customers who will not want to wade through something akin to *War and Peace*. Articles can be of any length but generally anything from 500 to 1,500 words is a good rule of thumb about size. If you need to write more than this on a particular theme, break it into a series of articles by calling them Part 1, Part 2 and so on.

You can publish your article(s) on your own website, which is always a good tactic as it provides fresh content to your website. Search engines will rank higher any website that has regular updates or fresh content.

Another benefit of writing articles is that you can submit them to websites that specifically cater for this. Some of the most popular article directories are:

- www.ezinearticles.com

- www.articlesbase.com

- www.buzzle.com

- www.articledashboard.com

- www.isnare.com

There are hundreds of article directories that you could submit your articles to. However, the effort required to do so would not be worthwhile. Stay with a few article directories and post to them regularly.

Many article directories enjoy a good reputation with the search engines and you can gain some of that reputation by getting your articles published on them. All article directories allow you to have a backlink or even two from your article back to your website. This is useful for boosting your website's ranking and it also allows readers of your article to find out more about you and your therapy with the possibility of them becoming customers.

When submitting articles to the different directories you have selected, it is worthwhile if you make each article slightly different in some way for each directory. This might mean that you change the article title and sub-headings within the article body. Changing the beginning of sentences at the start and ending of paragraphs helps too. This way you avoid duplicate content being recognised by search engines and each version of your article can stand alone.

Structuring an article

When writing an article choose a theme that you know or believe will be relevant to your customer base. A business coach whose target audience is sole traders might create an article with the title 'The Top Ten Small Business Mistakes' or 'Ten Things for Small Businesses to Avoid'.

Articles that have a list of 10 or 12 tips are often the easiest articles to compose and an easy structure for this type of article is:-

1. An introduction to the article and the problem you are addressing.
2. The ten tips.
3. A summary of the article and the importance of the 10 tips.

With any other article it can be useful to remember and follow a similar structure as set out below. To demonstrate this, examples of a business coach writing about small businesses and a therapist writing about arthritis are given:

1. Introduce what the article is about, e.g.:
   Small business mistakes
   An ailment such as arthritis

2. Describe the problem – give a short description about it, e.g.:
   Small business – working long hours, inefficient work practices, no business plan
   Arthritis – what it is and what the different types are

3. Describe what you know is desired by someone who has this problem, e.g.:
   Your business will enjoy bigger profits, be more efficient, be able to expand
   Arthritis – your body moves more easily and with less pain

4. Describe how your expertise or skill can help with this problem but do not write blatant advertising copy. Citing relevant research that agrees that your therapy can help with the problem will start to build the potential client's trust and confidence in you.

5. Summarise your article

6. Author's details. Include your name, your professional title (e.g. Reiki Practitioner), your location and your website (depending on the article website's rules, you may be able to include your email address and a second website link).

You can get a lot of mileage from writing one article. By composing a number of variations of that one article you can publish it on a number of websites with different titles and this will help to avoid it being seen as duplicated content. Article writing takes time but its rewards are worth the effort.

83

PARTICIPATING IN EGROUPS AND FORUMS

Being a therapist can be quite a lonely occupation. Even those therapy association annual conventions or quarterly chapter meetings may not provide enough contact to help ease the notion that as a therapist, you are more often than not, on your own.

With the advent of easier communications on the internet, you can have more contact with like-minded therapists without having to wait for that physical meeting every three months or once a year.

There are now thousands of egroups that are listed by subject that you can join. These egroups can be on any topic ranging from student life in Huddersfield to the study of the life cycle of the cabbage white butterfly. Lawyers, dentists, mechanics can all have, and do have, their own egroups.

Thousands of Egroups can also be found under general categories such as health, business, computers, sport, relationships, religion, education, music, hobbies, government and more. With this in mind there are hundreds of egroups that have been established for specific complementary therapies and coaching.

If you play an active role by giving advice or just providing information on your area of expertise, you can build up a healthy reputation for yourself. If, when you respond to any email, you also include details of your website, you will attract surfers and new clients. There is no cost to join an egroup other than your time but the reward can be more clients.

Although egroups and forums enable you to stay in touch with other therapists and coaches they also enable you to interact with potential customers and clients. Some forums and egroups have a very focused theme, such as trichotillomania (compulsive hair pulling). If you become a member of this group and are able to provide useful tips and strategies, you will build yourself an important reputation. You will be perceived a source of knowledge and if your therapy is able to offer help with the specific issue of that group, you will gain new customers. Once again it is important to be subtle and give value, rather than be blatant about your business needs.

Finding forums and egroups

Often your own therapy or coaching associations will provide this as way of sharing experiences, expertise and offering guidance for you and other members.

To find forums and egroups where specific ailments, issues and problems are discussed you can search the egroups provided by Yahoo:

www.yahoogroups.com

To find forums on the internet, simply type into any search engine the words 'ailment forum' (e.g. Arthritis forum). You will then see a list of forums which all have the ailment you have specified as a core theme. You just need to sign up and confirm your membership and then you can start posting your comments and thoughts.

When you are a new member of a forum or egroup, take it easy with your posts and be supportive of other members' comments and postings. Do not dive in immediately and state that you can help to cure anything or that anyone with any issue can be helped by seeing you. No one likes obvious sales patter and you will lose more than you gain if you take this approach.

Each forum will have rules that you must adhere to if you want to remain a respected member. Most forums will allow you to enter your website address in the signature element of your membership profile. This is a subtle way of letting the members know you have an area of expertise and if your comments and posts provide value, you will find people want to find out more about you and your business by clicking on the website link in your signature box. Your signature is automatically added to any post you make.

Running your own forum or egroup

Finally, setting up your own forum or egroup can be an effective marketing strategy. You can easily set up a new egroup at Yahoo groups once you are a member. Setting up a forum is a bit more challenging but you may find that your web hosting company already provides this facility for you or can guide you on how to add it to your website.

84

SHARING YOUR EXPERTISE

There are websites now that encourage visitors to ask questions connected to some issue or life challenge or websites that enable you to answer perceived information needs. These life challenges or information needs can range from 'How do I change a fuse in a plug?' to 'How do I quit smoking?'.

Other members of these websites will then answer the question. Some questions may receive no answers at all but most receive a number of responses. Sometimes the person who posed the original question or other members, will also be able to vote for the answer to a question that they judge is the most helpful.

Some of the most popular websites are:

■ www.yahooanswers.com – on this website members ask questions and wait for answers.

157

- www.answerbag.com – questions are asked and any number of members can respond.

- www.ehow.com – on this website members anticipate the information needs of others. They do this by providing answers to the 'how to' type of questions.

Participating on these websites and others of a similar nature can again enhance your reputation and provide a source of new customers. The more value you manage to give in your answers or information, the more trust you will receive and as a result, increase the customers you can attract. It is also possible to include links to your website. If you have a resourceful article that you believe can help, you could give the link to it in your response.

If you are thinking about writing an article, you can research the subject of your new article by using the websites above. If you discover that members have been asking questions that can be connected to your therapy you could use this opportunity to market your services. Just write an article that answers those questions you have researched, then publish it on your website. Go back to those websites previously listed and give a short answer to the questions you previously found and then provide a backlink to the fuller answer (your article) that is published on your website.

85

BLOGGING YOUR SERVICES

A blog is like an internet version of a diary, or at least that was its original intention. People who wrote in a blog used it to describe events that had happened to them in chronological order. For example, someone who is pregnant for the first time might describe their life as an expectant mother culminating in the birth of their child. Another person's blog might be on the subject of their experiences as they travel round the world.

The search engines love fresh content. The very nature of blogs means that they have regular updated content. So search engines tend to favour these blogs in their search rankings. Internet marketers also recognised the opportunity for marketing any service or product via a blog.

Many internet host companies provide the facility to attach a blog to your website. You can contact them to find out if this is an option for you. If they don't do this already you have a few other options which are:

1. Pay an extra fee to have a blog attached to your website (contact your hosting company).
2. Buy a new domain name and have it hosted by a company that does provide a blog facility.
3. Use one of the free blogging platforms.

The best option is to have your blog attached to or as part of the same domain that your therapy or coaching business uses. Although you choose any name you want to, typically the address of your blog could be:

www.yourtherapy.co.uk/blog

The second best option is buying a new domain name from a hosting company that provides a blog facility. If you choose to do this your blog address could simply be:

www.yourtherapy.co.uk

A free blogging hosting and domain name can be effective too. You can find the two most popular free platforms for blogging at these addresses:

www.blogger.com
www.wordpress.com

Wordpress is probably the most popular choice for a free blogging website. You will be able to choose a domain name (as long as it hasn't been taken already) and choose from hundreds of design templates.

Getting the most from your blog

If you decide to obtain a blog, you must write articles (referred to as 'posts') to your blog on a reasonably regular basis. Blog posts can be short (just a paragraph) or they can be lengthy. Remember who your audience is and whether they will want to plough through a long article or not. If you write posts between 250 and 500 words, you should be able to communicate the salient points of the article, make it an easy read and provide enough information to create value for your blog.

It is better to author regular short articles every two weeks, than lengthy articles every month. If you manage to write one article every two weeks you will encourage the search engines to visit your blog because it has fresh content.

Just like writing articles, the structure of your posts will follow a similar order. Think of a good title for your post and then write an introduction, give the thrust of the article's subject and then make a conclusion.

Previously in this chapter, the importance of keywords or keyword phrases has been emphasised. Keywords are important to blogs too but they are referred to as 'tags'. When you see the facility to add new tags to any blog posting, just think of your keywords and add them.

Connecting blogs to websites

You will want to gain the maximum return for all your blogging efforts. Make it as easy as possible for the visitors to your blog to be able to either contact directly from your blog or to be able to navigate quickly to your website.

You can achieve this by having contact details (website, email address and telephone number) on every page of your website and/or have these are the bottom of every post that you write. This is often referred to as an author's resource box (you will have one on the article directory websites) and it can look like this:

Authored by: Fred Bloggs

Certified Aromatherapist – Glasgow   Tel: 0141 000 000

Website: www.aromatherapy-glasgow.net

Email: info@aromatherapy-glasgow.net

Some bloggers also include a head and shoulders photograph with this type of author resource box to help build the relationship between the reader and the blogger (therapist or coach).

Comments and spam

Blogs allow for interaction between the blog visitor and the blogger. When a visitor reads a post on a blog they can leave a comment about their opinion of that article. This is another great asset of having a blog as search engines view comments as fresh content on your blog. This saves you some work as it means you don't have to write all the fresh content to your blog.

Most comments are positive and appreciative of the post you have written. Occasionally someone can leave negative comments. Don't be too quick to delete negative comments. Negative comments may start an interesting discussion between you and the commenter and draw in others to leave their opinion too which in turn gains you more fresh content.

Ultimately you retain control of whether you allow comments to be shown on your blog. Some comments are considered to be spam. These comments will be relatively easy to spot as they will be very generalised such as 'nice post' or 'great blog' or some other comment that does not have any connection to your post. The people who leave such comments are after a backlink from your blog to their website and they can get this by leaving a comment. If a comment shows that they have read your post and provided a useful opinion then it is worthwhile keeping that comment and you also get the chance to respond to it in a comment that you make. However, if it looks like a spam comment, then delete it.

Keep to a pace of posting to your blog that suits your time and writing abilities. If you don't find writing comes easily you can aim for short and more frequent posts. Try to be consistent about the frequency of posting too as this helps the search engines to know when to visit your blog to find fresh content.

Blog directories

You can submit your blog's address to many directories which is another way of letting others know about your blog content and your business. Here are some blog directories that you can add your blog to:

- www.blogcatalog.com
- www.bloggernity.com
- www.technorati.com
- www.bloghub.com
- www.blogged.com

RSS – Really simply syndication

With blogs being a major source of content, they are of value to those websites whose business it is to provide news, articles, opinions and other types of new content. RSS directories provide a syndication service which takes the content of your blog and makes it available for publication to other websites.

The benefits of this to you are that you get exposure for your articles and your business, to a wider community and bigger audience. You also gain backlinks to your blog which help its search engine ranking.

The content of your website will need to be in a form or structure that RSS directories can read. This form or structure is referred to as feed. You will need to check on the address of your RSS feed because this feed address is needed when you want your blog's content to be distributed by an RSS directory. Typically your blog's RSS feed address will look like one of these examples:-

www.yourtherapy.com/feed
www.yourtherapy.com/feed/rss

If you have used Wordpress or Blogger for your blog, there will be a help section where you can find out the address for your blogs RSS feed.

RSS directories

Armed with your RSS address now you need to add it to various RSS directories. There are thousands of directories so you won't be able to add it to all the directories that exist. A few of the top RSS directories can be found by typing 'RSS directories' into any search engine. Here are some of popular RSS directories:

- www.feedage.com

- www.palzoo.com

- www.weblogalot.com

- www.5z5.com

- www.feedburner.com

It can prove rewarding to get into the habit of submitting your RSS feed to new directories. Some directories require you to open a free account and have a user-id and password. Keep a record of these or use a memorable naming convention just in case you need to revisit these sites and add more feeds from another website. Many directories allow you to submit your RSS address without having to open an account.

Blogs add a new dimension to any business's web presence. They are an effective means of promotion and enable interaction between a visitor, other visitors and you. Interaction is the start of a relationship and gives you an opportunity to build that vital emotional sense called trust.

86

BACKLINKING TO RANK HIGHER

On any website you will find a navigation menu which enables you to perform a mouse click on a button, text or image that takes you to another page within the website. This is called a link and this is the means by which your website's pages are connected to each other.

A backlink is when another website has a link to your website. Your therapy or coaching association's website will often provide a link from their website to your website. Your association is providing a backlink to your website.

Backlinks are therefore links from other businesses, organisations, forums, directories or other websites to your website.

Search engines calculate how well your website is ranked based, partly, on the backlinks to your website. There are other factors that play a part in your search engine ranking but backlinks are one of the most vital elements of ranking well.

Many of the previous tips in this chapter provide ideas on how to get backlinks to your website. These include:

1. Submitting your website to directories.
2. Participating in forums.

3. Answering and asking questions on 'how to' websites.
4. Having your own blog.
5. Submitting your RSS feed to RSS directories.
6. Authoring articles for publication to article directories.
7. Networking on social network websites.

All these provide opportunities to link to your website and help improve its search engine ranking. There are other ways in which you can give a boost to promoting your website too.

The importance of anchor text

Many website owners gain backlinks from other websites but make the mistake of making their website address the text that is clickable. In other words, they make www.yourtherapy.com the words that need to be clicked on to get to their website. Search engines view the text, called 'anchor text' as another way of discovering the keywords that are important to your website.

Rather than have your domain name as the anchor (clickable) text, try to make some of your keywords clickable. An example would be:

Reflexology in Huddersfield

Any visitor that clicks on the above text will still be taken to your website; however, the search engines will be able to recognise that those words 'Reflexology in Huddersfield' are keywords for your business. This will help your website to rank higher when anyone uses the keywords to find a reflexogist in Huddersfield.

Try to use a number of variations on your keywords in the anchor text of backlinks such as:

Huddersfield Reflexologist
Reflexology in West Yorkshire
Reflexologist in West Yorkshire
Reflexology in Huddersfield

Other sources for backlinks

The tip about building a blog mentioned that visitors can comment on your blog posts. When they do this, they also get the chance to enter the address of their website. If you approve that comment, a backlink is created between your blog and their website. You get free content in the form of a – hopefully – positive and useful comment and they get a backlink.

With this in mind, you too can also obtain backlinks by visiting other blogs and leaving a comment for them and adding your website address. Bear in mind that they will moderate their blog comments and if your comment appears spammy or of little value they will delete it. When you make a comment refer to the blog post you are commenting on and offer an opinion or make other positive suggestions. Give value in your comment and the blog owner is more likely to approve your comment and your reward will be another backlink.

Bookmarking websites

Some websites have been set up with the aim of allowing members to bookmark other websites. These allow you to have backlinks to your website(s) and even to an internal page of your website where you may have written an article. All these bookmarking websites are free, just requiring that you open an account with them.

Here are some of the most popular bookmarking websites:

- www.reddit.com
- www.stumbleupon.com
- www.digg.com
- www.delicious.com
- www.mixx.com
- www.slashdot.com

You can also add the address of your blog to these websites.

Reciprocal linking

As the term 'reciprocal' suggests, this is a form of bartering or swapping links. Most websites will have, as one of their internal pages, a link page listing other businesses or personal websites. Many therapists and coaches have a links page and have approached other therapists or coaches and asked to swap links.

When they do this, although the search engines want you to have backlinks from similar themed sites, which they view as a kind of popularity vote, any gain you achieved by getting a backlink can be cancelled out by giving a link back.

By all means have some reciprocal linking between your website and your therapy colleagues' websites but do not make this a priority over other linking tactics.

PR websites

Press release (PR) websites enable you to announce to the internet world the arrival of your new business or the launch of some change to your business. A launch might be a new way of using your therapy; it might be that you now will specialise in a particular ailment or you have just opened up new premises. If you have opened up new premises, while this may be exciting for you, it may fall into the 'so what?' mentality for others. If you have new premises by all means create a press release but in addition include what will be different or special or unique about what you will offer your customers from your new premises.

Any newsworthy story you can create can give you a good reason for submitting an internet press release. Some press release websites charge a fee for their service. Many sites are free and in putting together your press release you will be able to gain a backlink to your website.

Constructing a press release is different from writing an article. It needs to be short, punchy and create intrigue and even excitement. One A4 page should be sufficient for all the details you need to communicate and you should write in the third person, just as though you are talking about someone else's business. Never use the 'I' pronoun, always use your business name.

You can include adjectives such as: professional, experienced, qualified, expert, skilled, successful, effective, recognised, acknowledged, but avoid waffle, fluff and obvious hype. Don't overuse these words and avoid turning your release into an advertisement . . . well at least a blatant advertisement.

If anything, play down hype but create interest and intrigue instead. For example, a few years ago a Spanish hypnotherapist recreated the gastric band bypass surgery using hypnosis only. The fact that his client reacted to the suggestion via hypnosis, that a gastric band had been fitted in her stomach (even though it hadn't and she knew this consciously), and she lost many stones in weight, created intrigue. The story soon spread and was published in the national newspapers in the UK and elsewhere.

Although your aim is not necessarily for national publicity (yet) the above example grabs the attention and intrigues the reader.

Typically, the structure for a press release could be:

1. Headline – make this punchy and intriguing.
2. Add subheadings – they help those who like to skim read and provide a break from too much text.
3. First paragraph – this is the what, where, when and who.
4. Subsequent paragraphs – state a problem that your service addresses.
5. If possible have a quote from a happy customer.
6. Last paragraph – this is your call to action – tell the reader what to do next, such as go to your website, phone or email you.

Here are some free PR websites:

- www.betanews.com
- www.prleap.com
- www.prlog.org

■ www.openpr.com

■ www.sbwire.com

Use press releases sparingly, otherwise your efforts will be viewed as spammy and you may get the backlink but little else.

87

AUTOMATING CUSTOMER CONTACT

If you wait for customers to come to your website and contact you, any communication will be 'customer driven' and you, as the business owner have no control over this communication.

However, there is a marketing strategy of wresting that control from visitors or potential customers to your website so that you drive the communication.

If you have a website already you will know that a large proportion of your visitors will not contact you. These visitors are evidently interested in your services, hence their visit, but, for whatever reason, they are not committing themselves to taking the next step yet.

The problem is that when they are ready for your service, they might not be able to find your website again in the search engines and you could lose that customer to your competition.

It's useful to remember that marketing research has shown that it takes on average seven viewings (advert, poster, shop, website) of some service or product before a buying decision is made.

A potential client therefore may make several visits to your website or other websites before they make their buying decision. Although you have helped them with their research by having a website, they may make their buying decision when they are on your competitor's website. Likewise, if we take this marketing research literally, another client may have visited six of your competitors' websites and make their buying decision when they visit your website which just happens to be their seventh viewing or contact with your therapy.

Now, of course, while this research provides an average figure, and some people may make their buying decision on the first website they find, you can understand how many visitors you need to attract to your website before one of them makes a decision to contact you.

Part of the solution, excluding USPs such as a time-limited discount or free consultation, is to offer your visitors something of value for seemingly, nothing in return.

The 'something of value' might be:

1. Download a free self hypnosis recording.
2. Subscribe to our free health ezine.
3. Get a 6-part course on interview techniques.

The word 'free' is one of the most powerful words in marketing. Offering something of value for free is attractive to almost anyone who visits your website.

Any business which offers something for free is always after something in return. In this case, the valuable item you want in return is the visitor's email address. By collecting email addresses from your website visitors you gain a number of important advantages. You can:

1. Contact them when you want to.
2. Build a relationship with the customer.
3. Increase the contact if your client numbers are low.
4. Offer special incentives, discounts, deals.
5. Increase your client base by encouraging them to introduce a friend, family member or colleague.

There is no doubt that a customer who has been receiving regular contact from you that has been of value, is much more likely to choose you as their therapist or coach when they are ready to make their buying decision.

By employing this strategy you gain more control over contact with your website visitors.

Autoresponders

Collecting email addresses and sending out regular emails can be automated. There are free and paid-for versions of automated emailing services called autoresponders. Two autoresponder service providers that charge a monthly subscription are:

- www.getresponse.com

- www.aweber.com

Use the above providers' services when you know you are aiming to build a large list of subscribers (1,000 plus) and will email those subscribers regularly (once or twice a month as a minimum).

If you are just starting out to collect email addresses you can do this either with the help of your web hosting company or by downloading one of the free autoresponder softwares, available from the internet, such as: www.massmailingnews.com

If you want to know how powerful this marketing method is, just reflect on how many ezines and other offers you receive in your inbox from energy, telephone, supermarket, restaurant and internet providers, all enticing you to buy more.

88

RECORDING AUDIO, VIDEO AND PODCASTING

Communication of an idea, information or an opinion can come in many forms. Words or text in written form are great for stating facts and data. Depending on your writing and grammar skills and vocabulary range, it is possible to convey more than just cold hard facts. With an effective use of adjectives it is possible to convey to the reader a sense or even feeling from that descriptive text.

One of the most powerful words that is used in marketing to help a potential customer get a better idea of what a new product or service would be like for them is the word 'imagine'. For example: 'Imagine being on a beach, with waves splashing and the sun warming your body. Imagine releasing any stress easily and feeling calmer and more relaxed'. When you use the word 'imagine' the reader is compelled to imagine and then start to experience the sensations and feelings you are describing.

Yet text can still be akin to a two-dimensional way of communicating. It is said that a picture or image can better a thousand words. The right image can communicate so much more than words can do. It is important to include images on your web pages for this reason.

Whenever possible use other forms of communicating with your customers. These other forms, including audios and videos, will help you to form a relationship with a customer more easily than words alone.

Audio recordings

Recording a welcome message for your website visitors adds an extra dimension to your internet marketing. Just like the telephone enables two people to build or maintain a relationship through listening to how someone speaks, recording your voice and creating an audio file will provide that same opportunity to build the start of the client and therapist relationship.

A short message of welcome that introduces yourself and includes a USP (Unique Selling Proposition) with a relaxed and easy-going tone will encourage customers to go that extra step and contact you.

Don't make the mistake of cramming in too much information and speaking too fast. A short message in a relaxed voice will prove more effective than overwhelming the customer with facts.

With audio files that are embedded in your website you can choose to have them play automatically when a visitor arrives at your website or you can allow your visitor to choose to play the recording or not.

Remembering that some customers access your website in public places such as their work environment or an internet cafe it may be best to allow the customer the choice to play the recording.

Video recordings

If audio recordings help to add a different dimension to internet marketing, video recordings go a step further. With the relationship being an important factor in choosing a therapist or coach, a video can help a customer gain a better sense of how you are as a person and therapist, than any other medium.

A customer not only gets to hear your voice, they get to see you in person and watch how you explain and describe yourself, your practice and how you operate. They will pay attention to your mannerisms and will also take note of the environment that the video was shot in.

You want to come across as both relaxed and friendly but professional too. Dress as you would do for your client sessions. If possible have the video shot in your practice or therapy room and make sure it looks professional and uncluttered too.

Submitting your video to video directories and websites can also attract more traffic (visitors) to your website.

Here are some websites that you can upload your video to:

- www.youtube.com

- www.video.google.com

- www.dailymotion.com

- www.metacafe.com

When producing audio and video recordings it is important to write a script or at least have a structure to your message. Rehearse it a few times until it flows and you are happy that you have included all the information that is important. Again keep your message simple and aim for a duration of three to five minutes.

Do not leave errors of speech in your recording. Edit them out or re-record your message. Take your time and talk at a pace that allows the listener to absorb the information.

Podcasting

Podcasting is the regular publication of audio and video files to the internet. It is about creating a series of recordings that you then make available for other people to hear or watch.

For example, as a massage therapist you might provide a series of videos for parents on how to massage their baby. As a coach you could create a series of audio recordings on how to conduct yourself at an interview and increase the odds of getting that job.

You could also turn any articles you have written already into an audio or video version of that information.

Here are some podcasting websites you can submit your audio or video creations to:

- www.podcastalley.com

- www.podcastdirectory.com

- www.apple.com/itunes/podcasts/

You can create reasonable quality audio and video files from your computer or laptop. An even better option is to use a digital camcorder or digital voice recorder and then download the results to your computer.

Recording your voice or videoing your self encourages the start of the relationship with your prospective clients. Submitting your video or audio files to other websites increases your marketing reach and will also gain you valuable backlinks too.

and finally . . .

It's appropriate to emphasise once more just how important staying up to date with the internet's development is as new websites continue to offer new opportunities. With this in mind you would be well-advised to utilise these websites:

- www.twitter.com

- www.facebook.com

- www.squidoo.com

- www.hubpages.com

Twitter encourages you to send messages no longer than 140 characters in length as frequently as you want to. Other members can choose to follow you and receive your messages which are referred to as 'tweets'.

Facebook is a major player in the social interaction family of websites. You can use your membership to make posts of value that can attract clients You can also choose to pay for advertising to a cross-section of members that are most likely to want your service.

Squidoo and Hubpages are similar in nature. They both offer the chance to construct websites for niche subjects or generalised subjects. These websites are constructed from modules, such as a video, text, amazon, audio modules and others. Together these modules form a website that you mantain.

All four of these websites and others are free to join and allow you to have backlinks to enable you to drive more traffic to your therapy or coaching website.

Don't be overwhelmed by the number of opportunities on the internet or in this chapter. Start off with the basics of having a great-looking website. Once your website is available, start to action those tips that help to improve your search engine rankings. After that you can gradually progress with the other tips in this chapter. You don't need to use all these tips but the more you use the better your results will be.

CONNECTING TO THE INTERNET

Businesses that fail to take advantage of up-to-date marketing methods will struggle. You need at least to match, if not stay ahead of, your rivals. History is littered with companies that refused to modernise for whatever reason or principle.

Offering Extra Enticers

Get past people's doubts and objections and you stand a better chance of turning an enquirer into a customer.

Aim to be different. Aim to stand out from the crowd or the common herd. If you are going to copy the competition you must improve on what they have done. Make your service as individual and different from the rest as possible.

Part of your uniqueness can be achieved by providing value beyond your customers' expectations. Giving extra value does not necessarily equate to more expense for you. In fact, in the long run, it can cut your marketing costs, as the clients that find you through 'word of mouth' will increase.

89

REWARDING RECOMMENDERS

As you become more and more established you will find that word starts to spread about how good you are. You will find people telephoning you for an appointment because a previous client has recommended you. This method of obtaining new clients is essential for any long-term business.

Personal recommendations are important because any business needs to build a solid reputation for the service it provides. A client who has been referred to you by someone else has more faith in your abilities than in those of a therapist who has been picked randomly from some directory. In effect they have had proof that you can get results, otherwise you would not have been recommended.

As the therapist, you have not had to spend any of your income on marketing to get this person as your client. This client arrives with the belief that because they know someone you have helped, you can help them also.

Some unique therapists are able to brag that they never advertise for clients and that all their clients find them through their reputation. This is an enviable position to be in, but for the majority of therapists word of mouth alone is unlikely to provide a sufficient number of callers. People who are willing to recommend you should be encouraged.

Take the opportunity to talk to your clients about the other ailments you can help, for example, backache. If that client then sees a friend or relative who has backache they are likely to talk about your service. If a past client sends you a number of new clients, do find a way of thanking them. This could be as simple as paying them a referral fee per client, or you may decide to offer them a complimentary session as a gesture of thanks. Even just a short letter thanking them for their efforts can be enough to encourage them to continue referring people to you. Every referred client enhances your reputation and reduces your marketing costs.

90

OFFERING DISCOUNTS

Never restrict yourself with your marketing ideas. If the large companies have a new way of encouraging people to try their product, play with the idea and see if you can copy their concept for your business.

Some clients will book an occasional therapy session every month or so. Others will want a series of sessions. It can be useful to know in advance how many clients you have next week, next month and even over the space of a year. Discounts can encourage the client to make definite dates for future sessions rather than coming on an ad hoc basis.

There are many strategies for making discounts work for you and numerous schemes to offer. The best for your practice may be the tried and tested favourite of 'Pay for five sessions in advance and get the sixth free'. This scheme means that you have payment before any sessions start and have future sessions booked. Another option is to give an existing client a discount voucher (e.g. 10% off) for a friend or relative or to encourage your clients to recommend you to others and reward them with discounts for every new client they send to you.

If you give out discount vouchers, always have a 'Use by' date on them. This helps the potential client to make up their mind to use your services sooner rather than later. It also means that you don't have hundreds of discount vouchers floating around that may turn up years later when you no longer need to use this strategy.

You may also consider giving discounts to specific groups of people. For example, you could offer anyone who works for the NHS a special Health Service discount. This focused discount strategy can help raise your profile among doctors, nurses and others in the caring professions.

91

SELLING GIFT VOUCHERS

As you might expect with this strategy, you simply sell gift vouchers that can be exchanged for therapy. This will not be applicable to certain therapies such as hypnotherapy or psychotherapy. If a friend or relative bought you a gift voucher to be redeemed at a psychotherapist's practice, you would consider it odd to say the least.

Selling gift vouchers will be more applicable for those such as aromatherapists, reflexologists, colour healers and others – if you like, the more physical type of therapies, as opposed to the mental and emotional therapies.

As with discount vouchers, always have a 'Use by' date. It would be considered fair to make the gift voucher valid for one year. Certainly other businesses such as booksellers issue gift certificates with a similar 'Use by' date.

In your practice room have a display of gift vouchers and mention these in your practice brochure. You may even suggest to your clients that an excellent and unusual Mother's Day gift is the chance to enjoy a wonderfully relaxing massage.

The only cost to you is the printing of the gift voucher. The advantages are that you get paid in advance whether the recipient uses the voucher or not. It is also a great way of increasing your client base and often the person who has been treated to a therapy will want to pay for more sessions themselves.

Just like tokens you can buy from booksellers, the gift voucher looks better if it is presented in a blank greetings card. The blank card allows the person giving the gift the space to write a personal message. You can charge a nominal amount for the card and envelope. This extra touch of providing cards and envelopes shows that you have given consideration to the presentation of the gift voucher to the recipient and adds to your client's perception of your professionalism.

92

OFFERING A FREE INITIAL CONSULTATION

Although many people will consider booking a session with you, a large percentage of these people will do nothing about it. They may take your leaflet and say to themselves that they will think about it later but never actually follow through and book an appointment. In effect, they have what is known in marketing circles, as an objection.

An objection is something that stops them from going ahead and paying for a session (or service, or product, etc.). They have a question or two which they would like to have answered before they will feel more comfortable about proceeding. A way of getting past that objection is to offer all your clients a free initial consultation.

A free consultation gives potential clients a chance to come along and meet you and ask their questions. They are not paying for this time and so they know that they have nothing to lose except their time. Although questions can be asked over the telephone or via email, people generally will not feel happy about parting with their money until they have met you in person and have those answers.

This does not necessarily apply to all therapies. It tends to be more relevant to talk therapies and particularly for help with mental and emotional issues. Having said that, not all 'talk' therapists offer a free consultation; some will charge for it. Often it is down to the therapist's personal choice. For the physical therapies, you will very rarely have to offer a free consultation. This strategy tends to be used by the new therapist to encourage the 'ditherer' to make up their mind. Once a client is sitting in front of you, and as long as you do not make a silly mistake, the majority will proceed into therapy after the consultation.

Reserving the next hour

For some therapists a successful strategy with free consultations is to make the following hour available so that the client can start their therapy immediately. If the client leaves after the consultation because you do not have the space in your appointments to start their first session, you risk the possibility of losing them and wasting the time that you gave them. Alternatively, by reserving an hour and a half for a client (e.g. consultation plus therapy session) you also risk them leaving after 30 minutes and wasting the following hour which you had kept clear just in case they wanted to proceed. Expect to lose time or clients no matter which strategy you use. You will find out the best procedure for you through trial and error.

Decide how long your free consultation will be and stick to it. Thirty minutes seems to be the popular choice. If you decide to keep the following hour free for your client make them aware of this before they arrive. If you inform them of this choice they are more likely to come prepared to take advantage of it. Using this method you will deal with any objections and it can become a USP (Unique Selling Proposition) for your practice.

93

GIVING FREE TALKS

Do not be afraid to provide free talks to the local community. Your library will sometimes have a room that they will let you use, or a community centre will allow you to provide free educational talks on the benefits of your therapy.

At schools, take the opportunity to talk to pupils who are looking for a career. Schools always invite accountants, computer programmers and engineers to talk about their careers, so take advantage of this opportunity and talk about your occupation. Tell them about your business and the fun you have. Provide leaflets for them to take away. Also give mini-demonstrations if you want them to get a flavour of your therapy. You will stick out like a sore thumb and be the talk of the school. Details of your talk and the therapy you offer will spread beyond the school gates and teachers to the parents.

This type of marketing costs you only your time and requires no expense other than the production of some extra leaflets. It increases your public persona and gets you talked about. New clients would rather see a therapist that they have heard something about (unless it is negative) than have to pick a complete unknown at random from a directory.

94

HOLDING OPEN DAYS

If you are a new therapist, or even an experienced therapist who has moved locations, you need to let as many people as possible know that you exist and what benefits you offer. A tried and tested method is to have an open day.

An open day is more applicable to a therapist who has rented or leased premises or a room in a complementary therapy practice. It would probably not be such a good idea for someone who practises from home.

The idea is to let everyone know that on a certain day between certain times your practice doors are open for the general public to come along and find out more about you and the therapy. This is the type of event where it is imperative to get the local newspapers, radio and even television stations involved. You will need the local media to run features on your practice and publicise the open day in advance. When the day arrives, you should encourage the local media to be there to see you interacting with potential customers and giving mini-demonstrations.

The media will want to photograph you with people. If necessary, persuade friends, neighbours and relatives to be there so that when the photographers or TV crew arrive you have people on whom you can demonstrate. Even if no one turns up for your open day, other than the people you know, you will still have gained some free publicity. If you give some incentive and have this mentioned in the announcement about the open day, you will persuade more people to turn up.

Ideas for incentives

- A free 10-minute demonstration on a strictly 'First come first served' basis

- Free 10-minute visualisation tape to the first 25 people

- Get a 20% discount voucher if you book your first session on the day

Have someone assisting you and offering everyone coffee or tea as they arrive. Put a few plates of biscuits or snacks around to encourage a relaxed, informal atmosphere. Have some background music playing and a pleasant aroma to add to the ambience.

This is your chance to make the open day a time for dealing with people's objections and allowing potential customers to meet you face to face. You get publicity which would ordinarily be very expensive and to make yourself known to the local community quickly.

OFFERING EXTRA INCENTIVES

Little things mean a lot. Develop an eye for adding that extra value that will enhance someone's experience of your therapy service.

Adding Miscellaneous Ideas

> The places, occasions and opportunities that a therapist can use to market their business are only limited by their imagination.

There is a whole raft of marketing ideas that you can take advantage of to bring yet more eager clients to your door.

Wherever you go, whether locally, nationally or abroad, always have your eyes peeled to spot how others promote themselves. It can be amazing how you can adapt tactics and strategies you have seen elsewhere to the marketing of your practice.

95

WORKING AT CRAFT MARKETS

All around the country, mainly at the weekend, but sometimes during the week, craft fairs and markets are organised. The goods on sale range from odd pieces of pottery to the usual knitting and weaving produce. There are stalls that sell natural medicines including herbal, homeopathic and Chinese medicines along with the Bach flower remedies. The description of 'craft' can be taken to mean any art, skill or creation.

At some fairs there will be Tarot Card readers, crystals and other gemstones will be for sale and possibly a medium will offer advice. There is nothing to stop any alternative or complementary practitioner setting up a stall and offering their services.

It is best to view this arena as a place to promote your therapy skills and your practice as opposed to giving a full session. However, you should be able to create mini-sessions or 'tasters' to recover your expenses for the day.

Examples of tasters

- Colour healer – give brief advice on the best colours for a person.

- Iridiologist – provide a brief analysis of someone's state of health.

- Crystal therapist – provide a check on the balance of the chakras.

- Acupressure therapist – manipulate some meridian points on the body in relation to a particular ailment.

All these ideas are intended to give a flavour of the type of treatment you offer and to arouse the curiosity of the general public. Make sure you make a nominal charge for these mini-sessions. You will often find that demonstrating your therapy on one person will attract others to gather round and watch. As with other strategies, always have plenty of leaflets to distribute and be prepared to accept bookings for your therapy.

96

TAKING A STALL AT A HEALTH FAIR

Events such as fairs are becoming more and more popular with the general public. At health fairs and mind–body–spirit events there is an enormous range of therapies, products and other services. With the more organised and national health fairs there are also guest speakers and mini-tutorials for attendees at extra cost.

The general set-up at a health fair is for therapists, course producers, natural medicine shops and a few others to hire stalls for a day or series of days to display what they have to offer. Many stall holders recover the cost of the day by offering mini-versions of their therapies. The product stalls will be selling oils, books, crystals and the like.

Appearing at the better fairs can be quite expensive so it can be worthwhile splitting the costs of a stall with a colleague. Two aromatherapists could operate on a shift basis – one could provide short therapy tasters to passing trade, and the other sell essential oils or oil burners. Another strategy is to get together and share a stall with someone who is offering a completely different therapy from you.

You might consider providing a tutorial at the fair. This is a great way of getting your name and therapy known and is likely to increase your chances of getting private clients. Just be clear about why you are taking a stall at the fair: Is it to earn some money while giving mini-sessions? Is it to encourage people to buy your latest self-help book, or to see you privately? Of course it could be a combination of all three, but if you are looking for private clients you will need the fair to be in your locality, whereas if you are selling products or your book it doesn't matter where the fair is located – within reason.

Initially, attend the fair as a customer to research how it is organised, the type of people who attend and the competition. Do your homework first and increase your chances of success.

97

PUBLICISING YOUR PRACTICE IN LIBRARIES

When they want some information that is not available in the home or through other means most people will turn to that central and vast source of information, the local library. This establishment can be another way for people to find out about you and an excellent addition to your marketing strategy.

There are two methods to adopt with regard to having a presence at your local library. One is the official way (with permission) and the other is the unofficial way (assumed permission).

With permission

The official way is to ask how you can add the details of your practice to the library's system. This will usually result in you being given a form to complete which will get you a listing on a local services directory on the computer. Do not expect to be inundated with clients from this source. It is worthwhile spending the few minutes it takes to get listed, but there are other more successful ways of using your library.

Ask if you may put a poster up giving details of your practice. Libraries have plenty of noticeboards. However, just because there is plenty of space available, doesn't necessarily mean that the head librarian will agree to your request. On most occasions they will refuse permission unless your poster includes something of interest to the local community. If you are giving free yoga classes to the over 65s or expectant mothers you are more likely to succeed. If the poster only promotes your private practice you will normally be refused. Give consideration to how to get past this hurdle if you want an official presence.

A compromise would be to describe your voluntary work and its time-table and also to include details of your private practice. Something along the lines of:

FREE YOGA CLASS

For the unemployed only
at
Bloggs Community Rooms
First Monday of each month
From 2pm to 3:30pm

Yoga can help you with
Stress, Memory and Concentration
For details telephone 597256

This does enough to satisfy the library's rules. The class you detail on the poster does not have to be something new. It can be something that you have been doing for some time. It is just a way of using what you are already doing to your best advantage.

Assumed permission

The unofficial approach is to assume you can put a poster up in the library. In other words, you do not ask permission. This does mean that it can become a 'cloak and dagger' operation – waiting for the right moment to place a poster when no one is looking! The only risk you take by doing this is one of the staff spotting you and telling you that you need permission to do it, or the staff noticing the poster and taking it down.

Using brochure stands

Another method and probably one with a greater response rate is using your practice brochure. Libraries have a number of brochure and leaflet holders which are crammed with details of local events, groups, societies, health matters, support groups and much more. All you need to do is place some of your brochures among these. The staff will not notice them but the users of the library will. This can be a very good source of new clients, particularly if you place leaflets in a number of different places within a library and at different libraries in the area.

In order to succeed in business, you do at times need to bend the rules a little. You are providing a worthwhile service and all you are doing is letting people know that you exist. That is what a library is for: providing information for the public about what is available to them.

98

ADVERTISING IN SPORTS CENTRES

A place where many people congregate or pass through each day is the local sports centre. People are at these centres to enjoy some physical activity and you can assume that they are interested in their health and in ways of staying healthy.

Capture their imagination and inform them what they will gain through your therapy and you will be rewarded with a crop of clients. Make it as easy as possible for them to find out about you. These centres always have carousels for holding leaflets about sports courses, classes and other events. They include leaflets detailing all the activities on offer at the centre. There will sometimes be other leaflet holders for leisure activities at places such as the local aerodrome, zoo and historical sites. Essentially, the facility to display your practice brochures is already provided. All you need to do is to fill it!

Some centres will not give you permission to display your brochures. Others will, if you create a link between a sports activity and your therapy. The centre management will be more accepting of your leaflets if there is the connection between what you are offering and the centre's activities. One of the easiest associations is for the therapist who offers help for sports injuries and highlights this fact in their leaflet.

If you can't find a direct connection between sports and your therapy you can still gain customers from sports centres. As long as there isn't a notice saying otherwise, then just place your leaflets in the racks. Keep them neat and tidy and don't go overboard. The idea is to attract customers but not to get the leaflets removed (by centre staff!). After some time of returning and restocking your leaflets as they get taken, you will find that the sports centre staff have also got used to seeing them there and will assume that permission has been granted for their display.

Focussing attracts clients

1. A Chinese herbalist can produce a leaflet stating how they can help with athlete's foot.
2. A shiatsu practitioner can highlight how they can help with energy levels.
3. A psychotherapist can connect physical fitness with mental and emotional fitness.

If your sports centre is really friendly you may even persuade them to display your posters in the café, reception area and locker rooms and anywhere there is a noticeboard.

99

GIVING AWAY PROMOTIONAL FREEBIES

If there was a way of reminding someone of your existence every day, it would be a great marketing strategy. If your contact details were always handy, then the possibilities of increasing your client base would greatly improve. Here is a possible way of achieving all of this.

At any opportunity, give your clients some promotional item which is of some benefit to them. The easiest item to give is a ballpoint pen. The pen is something the client can use but it also has a benefit for you. It includes your practice name and contact details. Every time that the pen is used your client is going to be reminded of you. If ever that client wants to pass on your details to someone else, all they have to do is reach for their pen. Although we lose pens all the time, in this particular case this loss can still work for you. We don't really lose pens as much as we leave them behind somewhere or lend them to other people and don't ask for them back. The good news is that a lost pen can generate more business for you. The new owner of the pen is going to see your details and may become a new client or pass it on to someone else.

Stationery companies have found ways of manufacturing these pens quite economically and so it won't cost you the earth to use this strategy. But a pen is just one example of a promotional freebie. With a little creativity you could give away many other items that all increase your client-attracting potential.

Examples of promotional items

- Key fobs
- Mugs
- Balloons
- Mouse mats
- Calendars
- Diaries

100

PRODUCING BOOKMARKS

A give-away that is relatively cheap to produce and can provide a fresh batch of clients for your practice is a bookmark.

Have printed on reasonably thick paper or material, probably a minimum of 120gsm, a vertical oblong shape sized approximately 8 inches by 1½ inches. If you turn an A4 sheet to landscape format, you can get 7 bookmarks. They look exactly the same as those many of the major bookshops give away when a customer buys a book. The customer gets a bag with the bookshop's name on it and a bookmark. Every time the customer uses that bookmark when reading their new book they will be reminded of the shop they bought it from.

Likewise, your bookmark will drop a hint about your therapy and all the benefits you can provide. You can distribute these to all your local libraries. Each time someone borrows a book they get one of your bookmarks. You could also drop some off at your local bookshops. Not all bookshops provide this service and so the smaller ones will appreciate this benefit for their clients. You might even be able to negotiate to share the costs with a friendly bookstore with your details on one side and the store's details on the other.

Consider other places that have a supply of books. Provide some to your local colleges and universities which all have libraries of their own. When students take the books home from college your bookmark will go with them and provide more chances of gaining new clients. Also consider hospitals, hospices and other places, as well as corporate libraries.

101

PUTTING FLYERS ON CAR WINDSCREENS

How many times when you have parked in a car park, has someone put a leaflet behind your wiper blade? The leaflet could advertise a party, a discount at a store, details of a local bazaar or any of a multitude of different events. Some people find these flyers annoying but they produce the same action from people: they have to pull the flyer out from under the wiper blade. Once they have it in their hand, curiosity dictates that they will take a quick look at its contents. Unless the design is good and appeals to the driver straightaway, the flyer ends up as rubbish very quickly.

If you decide to use this method of promotion you need to capture the imagination of the driver within five seconds. Use an emotionally charged headline. Depending on the type of problems you offer help with, here are examples that you could use:

Fed Up Being Stressed?

or

Learn How to Relax Anywhere, Anytime

or

Does Your Life Lack Purpose?

Your headline must be punchy and hit the target. The smaller detail on the flyer can go on to say what therapy you are offering and include any reasons to take action immediately. These can be time limited, such as '10% discount before 31 March' or 'Free relaxation tape with each session while stocks last!'. Don't forget a contact telephone number. You may not want to include your postal address.

With any large commercial concern, where the business involves serving people en masse, a car park will be provided.

Examples of places with car parks

- Council run car parks
- Supermarkets

192

- Fast food chains

- Golf clubs

- Hardware stores

- Cinemas and theatres

- Pubs and wine bars

Most flyer deliverers do not ask permission. They just get on with it. If a supermarket or other business telephones and asks you not to do this in their car park, then you can comply with their request. Until such time, you can carry on attracting clients.

You do not have to make special trips to all the car parks in the area, although this can be done if you want to blitz a place. Why not have some handy in your car? The next time you use a car park, just go around and distribute your flyers.

102

ATTRACTING PASSING TRADE

In this modern hi-tech age of computers, the internet and television we sometimes forget that some of the old trusted methods can still reap rewards.

Plaques help marketing

Lawyers, doctors, dentists, accountants and other professionals like to have some form of plaque at their place of business. In the past this has been brass and has been inscribed with the person's name, designations and profession and maybe a telephone number. These plaques are usually positioned near the front door of the business premises.

The purpose of the plaque can be twofold. First, for people who have booked an appointment it confirms that they have arrived at the correct address. It can also add to the professionalism that the client expects. Second, it may attract passing trade. Some businesses place their plaque at the first entrance to the property grounds such as the gate. Again, it serves to confirm that new clients have arrived at the correct address but also it advertises the type of business that operates at these premises. This could produce the effect that people passing the plaque may either call in to find out more, or make a note of the telephone number and call for details.

Therapists who operate from their own private residence will not want passing trade calling in without an appointment, or neighbours to know their business. If your home looks too much as if a business is being run from it, then the local authorities may want to charge you a business rate. So for therapists based at home a plaque will not be a good idea, but for the rest it is an acceptable form of promotion and, once purchased, will not drain any more funds from your marketing budget.

Other options

There are other ways of attracting people passing by your practice premises. Many shop retailers use a free-standing noticeboard to attract customers. They put this outside during business hours and bring it back in when closing for the day. This gives a better chance of informing people of your existence and location. It can be particularly essential if you operate from premises that do not have a shop front but only a single anonymous door leading to your practice. You will probably need to get permission from the local authorities before using a noticeboard as it will be standing on a pedestrian path. Again this is not an option for the home therapist.

103

ADVERTISING ON CARS

Next time you are in a car park have a look at the stickers that people put on their cars. In the UK these will mainly be placed on the windows.

They give free advertising to car insurers or holiday destinations and so on – or can be some humorous prose. How many times have you seen a beaten up old jalopy with the sticker saying 'My other car is a Rolls Royce'? These stickers do get noticed.

Marketing via other people's cars

Consider designing a tasteful sticker of your own. These can be placed on your car, your partner's, or friends' and relatives' cars. Every time you see a new client give them a sticker for their car. Every time you send a mail pack include a sticker. Stickers are cheap to produce and you will need to give quite a few away to see some reward.

The design of the sticker is very important. It needs to catch someone's eye quickly and get them to take action. Like any form of copy, it needs to have an emotional impact.

If you have a memorable telephone number, this can really make a difference with car stickers. Something like 0800 RELAX would be fantastic for many therapists but even something like 0800 93 83 73 can be just as successful. Most therapists will have their standard telephone number. In this case you will have to rely on someone having a good memory or of them going to the trouble of writing it down.

Signs on your car

In the US, you can obtain car plates that promote your business. Football fanatics may show which team they follow with a plate showing COWBOYS, for the Dallas Cowboys. Students may have a plate showing the university they attend. Why not promote your practice with a sign alongside your registration plate? Do check the vehicle authorities first though.

If you really feel bold, you can always invest in magnetic signs that stick to the two front doors of your car or people carrier. Whenever you go on a trip for shopping or to the cinema for example, you can put your magnetic signs up and your car becomes a mobile promotional vehicle. When you get back home, you simply take the signs off and your car becomes a normal private vehicle.

104

GIVING THEM MORE!

Your clients' trust in you and your therapy is priceless. Gaining your clients' trust means that you are only a short step away from gaining their belief in your skills. Belief counts for a lot in any aspect of life but is particularly useful in the healing profession. Incredible as it might seem, some clients arrive with no belief in your therapy. They are there because conventional medicine has failed them and you are a last resort. They have more hope than belief at this stage.

If we feel valued as individuals or collectively, it boosts our esteem. It helps us to believe that we matter. Help your client feel that they are the most important person in the world to you during the therapy session. If you make them your centre of attention they will feel valued.

Any client will have in mind a rough idea of what they expect to get for their money. Give them any less and they will begrudge the money they have spent. Give them more and they will feel happy and attach a greater value to your service.

Adding extra value to your service

If a client has booked for an hour and you haven't quite completed the therapy, give them a little extra time (if your schedule permits). Some therapists tell clients that a session lasts an hour but always give a 70-minute session. The client gets an extra 10 minutes and will come to the conclusion that you are more interested in helping them than your fee.

■ Provide your client with a complimentary cassette tape of relaxation music.

■ Provide a printout of 'tips and advice' that might also assist the resolution of a problem (e.g. a colonic irrigation practitioner might provide dietary tips to aid recovery from IBS).

- Give copies of internet articles to educate the client more about their condition.

- Offer telephone and/or email support at an agreed time. You might even be more proactive and telephone them to get a progress report.

The above examples illustrate how you can surpass your client's expectations of your service. Giving them something more than they expect adds value to your service in their eyes. The added value that they feel can lead to them having more of that powerful resource – belief.

Oh yes – I don't know if you have noticed, but this book is subtitled '101 tried and tested ways to attract and retain clients'. This is number 104! Do make sure your client notices the added extras, otherwise they will be wasted.

ADDING MISCELLANEOUS IDEAS

Wherever and whenever you visit a place or event that attracts a number of people make a game of spotting the ways vendors of all types use to attract business. Even the promotion of a product or service completely unrelated to your service, with a little creativity may provide useful ideas for you.

A Winning Strategy

Find out what works for your business and stick to it. Monitoring all aspects of your business is vital to its continued success.

In order to ensure a steady stream of enquiries, you should market your practice every week. That means *every* week. If you stop marketing when you are experiencing a feast of clients then you will soon experience a famine. Some marketing methods require a longer lead time to get a response, maybe weeks or months. Others can be rewarding very quickly – literally within hours. If you continue to market your practice every week you give yourself what every therapist craves: a reliable flow of new clients week after week and financial security.

Follow this A.C.T.I.O.N. formula:

Activity

What is the activity or action you need to do to promote your business?

Communicate

It is most important to get all aspects of your communication right. What message are you trying to communicate on the telephone, in a letter, when greeting clients to your practice, in your promotions?

Tenacity

Keep going. Persistence pays. While others may fall by the wayside, you will succeed by pursuing your marketing goals.

Inventive

Dare to be different. Don't only imitate what is good but improve on it. Use your creative skills in every task you tackle.

Opportunity

Be an opportunity taker. Look for the opportunities in everything you come across. You can make your own luck.

Now

Tomorrow never comes. Don't leave things so long that your ideas are actioned by someone else and you find yourself saying, 'I was thinking of doing that.' While you are thinking about it others may be doing it. Take action today!

If you get more enquiries than you can handle, you can always start a waiting list. Although your intention is to help people as soon as possible it is sometimes impractical to see everyone. If you have to start a waiting list it also adds to the perception of a therapist who is so successful that people are willing to wait to see them. Of course you can always refer your excess clients to colleagues. Your colleagues will think you are fantastic because you are giving them business and the client gets to see a therapist sooner.

Set your sights on attracting a certain number of clients each week and make the target achievable. As you reach a target set a new target until you attract the number of clients you are comfortable with each week. Never worry about over-marketing yourself.

Monitoring your marketing

Next to your accounting and client case histories, one of your most important administration tasks is to record how successful your marketing has been. Whenever you see a new client always ask them how they heard about you. This should be one of the questions on your case history form anyway. But don't leave that particular piece of information there. At the end of the week transfer the details of how your clients found you to your marketing monitoring records. This literally takes five minutes but can save you an amazing amount of time, energy and money.

Invest in a book of blank pages and head each page with details of the marketing method, the date started and how much, if anything, it cost you. For example:

Yellow Pages April 2011 to March 2012 Cost £1,200				**Page 1**
Date	*Client Name*	*Session Fee*	*Number of Sessions*	*Total*
03 Jan 11	Fred Smith	£70	1111 (4)	£280
04 Jan 11	Mary Bloggs	£70	11 (2)	£140
Library Leaflet	**April 2011**	**Cost FREE**		**Page 2**
Date	*Client Name*	*Session Fee*	*Number of Sessions*	*Total*
07 Feb 12	Joy Grange	£120	1 (1)	£120

From the above records you will soon see how well each marketing method is working for you. Keeping a total of the fees enables you to calculate quickly when you will be in profit with each method.

Keeping records of personal recommendations is also important because it acts as a notice from the client that they still remain very happy with the therapy they received from you. You may also want to drop them a note to thank them for their referrals. Your appreciation will encourage them to continue sending you more clients.

Analyse, adjust and repeat

Give each marketing method a set period for attracting clients. Once the period has ended, subtract the costs from the total of the clients' fees. You will then be left with either a profit, loss or break even figure.

If you have a profit then repeat this particular marketing strategy. If this strategy was a newspaper advertisement, for example, unless some aspect has been an obvious error, do not be tempted to change it significantly. Even though you may be bored with it because you have seen it so many times, the public will not have. In fact, even though this may be your second, third or fourth run of this advert, many people will be seeing it for the first time.

Strategies that break even may still be counted as one of your successes. Remember that the new clients who came to you through this may well recommend you to others in the future. So over a longer period of time you may find that this method moves from break even to profit. With break even strategies you should consider some minor changes but also consider running the promotion again as it is. Even some of the most successful strategies will, on occasions, bring in less than expected responses. This can be due to external factors like the season, Christmas, Easter, summer holiday time or other reasons.

With those strategies that disappoint – or in other words, do not pay for themselves – you should make wholesale changes before trying them out again. There is a strong possibility that with significant changes you can make this strategy a winning one. Some of the most successful marketing methods start out as the poorest but it is important to get as much value as possible from any strategy you use. The value from a strategy that fails is the lessons you learn.

It could be that a trade show costs you money and brings in very few customers. Rather than deciding that trade shows do not work, you must analyse how you ran your stall. Ask yourself questions like,

'What did I do that I could have done better?', 'What were my fellow stallholders doing?', 'Which stallholders seemed to be doing well and why?'. By answering these questions you may find solutions that will give you the confidence to attend another trade show – but this time be much better prepared.

When you have analysed every aspect of a particular marketing method that has not achieved the desired effect and you feel that no matter what you do, it never will, then drop it. Your winning marketing strategy must be to repeat what works for you, analyse and adjust what disappoints and drop what doesn't work.

Remember, it doesn't matter how fantastic a therapist you are, if potential clients don't know that you exist, your practice cannot be successful. Marketing is absolutely crucial to your business. Try out the ideas in this book, find which ones work best for you and add to them using your imagination. Good luck!

A WINNING STRATEGY

You cannot do everything at once. You should gradually roll out your marketing methods week by week.

Remember the saying 'The longest journey begins with the first step'.

Index

WITHDRAWN

184811